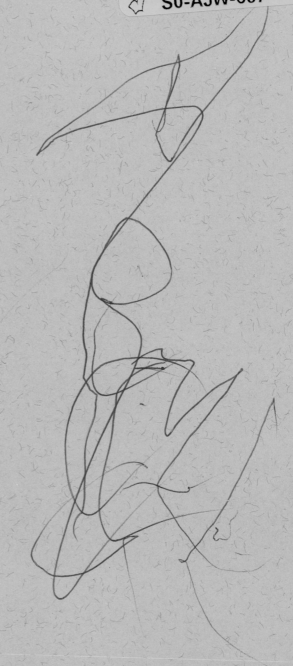

"Joseph Smith Seeks Wisdom from the Bible," by Dale Kilbourn.
Used by permission of The Church of Jesus Christ of Latter-day Saints.

BROTHER

JOSEPH

Stories and Lessons from the Life of the Prophet

COMPILED BY

KAY W. BRIGGS

Bookcraft
Salt Lake City, Utah

Library of Congress Catalog Card Number: 94-70826
ISBN 0-88494-905-2

First Printing, 1994

Printed in the United States of America

Contents

Acknowledgments

The history of Joseph Smith has been well preserved over the years by many of his friends and by some of his enemies. Many have taken the time to record the facts surrounding his life in an effort either to support his calling as a prophet of God or to condemn him as an impostor. The Briggs family would like to thank those who have tried, regardless of their point of view, to record accurately the many things that happened during his brief, thirty-eight-year life. The facts in this book are not original with us. They have all had some other source. We appreciate all those who have produced the many writings about this great man.

It has been said that more material has been written about the life of Joseph Smith, the Mormon Prophet, than any other American. In fact, some claim more has been written on his short lifetime than has been written about anyone other than the Lord and Savior, Jesus Christ. We cannot substantiate these claims, but through our research we have found a surprising number of books and other writings about his life.

So in this brief acknowledgment we thank all those who have written about him, regardless of motives or objectives. A special thanks is given to those authors whose names are found in the reference section at the back of this book.

The Briggs Family

"The First Vision," by Ted Henninger.
Used by permission of The Church of Jesus Christ of Latter-day Saints.

1

The Book of Mormon

I told the brethren that the Book of Mormon was the most correct of any book on earth, and the keystone of our religion, and a man would get nearer to God by abiding by its precepts, than by any other book.[1]

—Joseph Smith

"One of my descendants will revolutionize the world of religious faith"

The paternal grandfather of the Prophet was Asael Smith, a man of the strongest religious conviction. . . . Upon one occasion before the Prophet Joseph's birth, Asael Smith had a premonition that one of his descendants would be a great teacher and leader of men. To quote his words, as they are remembered and recorded by one who knew [him] and heard him speak: "It has been borne in upon my soul that one of my descendants will promulgate a work to revolutionize the world of religious faith."

It is not known if the young Joseph ever learned of this prophetic declaration until after his own career had been made manifest. But Asael lived to see the dawn of fulfilment of his words. Just before his death, the Book of Mormon, then recently printed, was presented to him. He accepted it, and with the light of inspiration which sometimes illumines the mind of man as the veil of eternity opens to his gaze, Asael solemnly warned his attendants to give heed to the book, for it was true, and its coming forth heralded a renewal of the gospel light.[2]

The visitations of the angel Moroni

The vision of the Father and the Son eventually proved to be only the first of many visions that the Prophet received, but he had to wait over three years for his next instructions from a heavenly messenger. He recorded this special event as follows:

> I continued to pursue my common vocations in life until the twenty-first of September, one thousand eight hundred and twenty-three, all the time suffering severe persecution at the hands of all classes of men, both religious and irreligious, because I continued to affirm that I had seen a vision. . . .
>
> . . . I often felt condemned for my weakness and imperfections; when, on the evening of the above-mentioned twenty-first of September, after I had retired to my bed for the night, I betook myself to prayer and supplication to Almighty God for forgiveness of all my sins and follies, and also for a manifestation to me, that I might know of my state and standing before him; for I had full confidence in obtaining a divine manifestation, as I previously had done.
>
> While I was thus in the act of calling upon God, I discovered a light appearing in my room, which continued to increase until the room was lighter than at noonday, when immediately a personage appeared at my bedside, standing in the air, for his feet did not touch the floor.
>
> He had on a loose robe of most exquisite whiteness. It was a whiteness beyond anything earthly I had ever seen; nor do I believe that any earthly thing could be made to appear so exceedingly white and brilliant. His hands were naked, and his arms also, a little above the wrist; so, also, were his feet naked, as were his legs, a little above the ankles. His head and neck were also bare. I could discover that he had no other clothing on but this robe, as it was open, so that I could see into his bosom.
>
> Not only was his robe exceedingly white, but his whole person was glorious beyond description, and his countenance truly like lightning. The room was exceedingly light, but not so very bright as immediately around his person. When I first looked upon him, I was afraid; but the fear soon left me.
>
> He called me by name, and said unto me that he was a

messenger sent from the presence of God to me, and that his name was Moroni; that God had a work for me to do; and that my name should be had for good and evil among all nations, kindreds, and tongues, or that it should be both good and evil spoken of among all people.

He said there was a book deposited, written upon gold plates, giving an account of the former inhabitants of this continent, and the source from whence they sprang. He also said that the fulness of the everlasting Gospel was contained in it, as delivered by the Savior to the ancient inhabitants;

Also, that there were two stones in silver bows—and these stones, fastened to a breastplate, constituted what is called the Urim and Thummim—deposited with the plates; and the possession and use of these stones were what constituted "seers" in ancient or former times; and that God had prepared them for the purpose of translating the book.
. . .

Again, he told me, that when I got those plates of which he had spoken—for the time that they should be obtained was not yet fulfilled—I should not show them to any person; neither the breastplate with the Urim and Thummim; only to those to whom I should be commanded to show them; if I did I should be destroyed. While he was conversing with me about the plates, the vision was opened to my mind that I could see the place where the plates were deposited, and that so clearly and distinctly that I knew the place again when I visited it.

After this communication, I saw the light in the room begin to gather immediately around the person of him who had been speaking to me, and it continued to do so until the room was again left dark, except just around him; when, instantly I saw, as it were, a conduit open right up into heaven, and he ascended till he entirely disappeared, and the room was left as it had been before this heavenly light had made its appearance.

I lay musing on the singularity of the scene, and marveling greatly at what had been told to me by this extraordinary messenger; when, in the midst of my meditation, I suddenly discovered that my room was again beginning to get lighted, and in an instant, as it were, the same heavenly messenger was again by my bedside.

He commenced, and again related the very same things

which he had done at his first visit, without the least varia-
tion; which having done, he informed me of great judgments which were coming upon the earth, with great deso-
lations by famine, sword, and pestilence; and that these
grievous judgments would come on the earth in this generation. Having related these things, he again ascended as he
had done before.

By this time, so deep were the impressions made on my
mind, that sleep had fled from my eyes, and I lay overwhelmed in astonishment at what I had both seen and
heard. But what was my surprise when again I beheld the
same messenger at my bedside, and heard him rehearse or
repeat over again to me the same things as before; and
added a caution to me, telling me that Satan would try to
tempt me (in consequence of the indigent circumstances of
my father's family), to get the plates for the purpose of getting rich. This he forbade me, saying that I must have no
other object in view in getting the plates but to glorify God,
and must not be influenced by any other motive than that
of building his kingdom; otherwise I could not get them.

After this third visit, he again ascended into heaven as
before, and I was again left to ponder on the strangeness of
what I had just experienced; when almost immediately after
the heavenly messenger had ascended from me for the third
time, the cock crowed, and I found that day was approaching, so that our interviews must have occupied the whole
of that night.

I shortly after arose from my bed, and, as usual, went to
the necessary labors of the day; but, in attempting to work
as at other times, I found my strength so exhausted as to
render me entirely unable. My father, who was laboring
along with me, discovered something to be wrong with me,
and told me to go home. I started with the intention of
going to the house; but, in attempting to cross the fence out
of the field where we were, my strength entirely failed me,
and I fell helpless on the ground, and for a time was quite
unconscious of anything.

The first thing that I can recollect was a voice speaking
unto me, calling me by name. I looked up, and beheld the
same messenger standing over my head, surrounded by
light as before. He then again related unto me all that he
had related to me the previous night, and commanded me

to go to my father and tell him of the vision and commandments which I had received.

I obeyed; I returned to my father in the field, and rehearsed the whole matter to him. He replied to me that it was of God, and told me to go and do as commanded by the messenger. I left the field, and went to the place where the messenger had told me the plates were deposited; and owing to the distinctness of the vision which I had had concerning it, I knew the place the instant that I arrived there.

Convenient to the village of Manchester, Ontario county, New York, stands a hill of considerable size, and the most elevated of any in the neighborhood. On the west side of this hill, not far from the top, under a stone of considerable size, lay the plates, deposited in a stone box. This stone was thick and rounding in the middle of the upper side, and thinner towards the edges, so that the middle part of it was visible above the ground, but the edge all around was covered with earth.

Having removed the earth, I obtained a lever, which I got fixed under the edge of the stone, and with a little exertion raised it up. I looked in, and there indeed did I behold the plates, the Urim and Thummim, and the breastplate, as stated by the messenger. The box in which they lay was formed by laying stones together in some kind of cement. In the bottom of the box were laid two stones crossways of the box, and on these stones lay the plates and the other things with them.

I made an attempt to take them out, but was forbidden by the messenger, and was again informed that the time for bringing them forth had not yet arrived, neither would it, until four years from that time; but he told me that I should come to that place precisely in one year from that time, and that he would there meet with me, and that I should continue to do so until the time should come for obtaining the plates. (Joseph Smith—History 1:27, 29–35, 42–53.)

Joseph described the ancient inhabitants of America as if he had spent his whole life among them

Lucy Mack Smith, Joseph's mother, described how Joseph would teach the family nightly about the things he had seen and heard from the Lord:

> Joseph commenced telling us the great and glorious things which God had manifested to him. . . . From this time forth, Joseph continued to receive instructions from the Lord, and we continued to get the children together every evening for the purpose of listening. . . . I presume our family presented an aspect as singular as any that ever lived upon the face of the earth—all seated in a circle, father, mother, sons and daughters, and giving the most profound attention to a boy, eighteen years of age, who had never read the Bible through in his life. . . .
>
> During our evening conversations, Joseph would occasionally give us some of the most amusing recitals that could be imagined. He would describe the ancient inhabitants of this continent, their dress, mode of traveling, and the animals upon which they rode; their cities, their buildings, with every particular; their mode of warfare; and also their religious worship. This he would do with as much ease, seemingly, as if he had spent his whole life among them.[3]

"I feel . . . relieved of a burden which was almost too heavy for me to bear"

Finally a long-awaited day came. The translation of the Book of Mormon plates was completed. Joseph Smith wanted those who cared for him to be present at the Whitmer farm in Fayette. His father was there, his mother, Oliver Cowdery, Martin Harris, and the Whitmers. He told Oliver Cowdery he would be one of the witnesses and David Whitmer would be another. And then, approaching Martin Harris, he said, "Martin Harris, you have got to humble yourself before God this day, that you may obtain a forgiveness of your sins. If you do, it is the will of God that you should look upon the plates, in company with Oliver Cowdery and David Whitmer."[4]

The four left the house and went to the woods. They knelt and began to pray, praying vocally in turn. After each one had prayed twice, Martin Harris arose and said, "It is my fault that our prayers are not answered," and then he left. Shortly after his departure, a brilliant light appeared and an angel stood before them holding the plates and turning some of the leaves. They all heard the voice of God speak from the heavens bearing witness that the translation was correct.

After the vision closed, Joseph Smith went to find Martin Harris. He found him praying. He knelt with him, and they prayed together. The same vision was opened to them. They beheld an angel, saw the plates, and heard the voice of God. Martin Harris was soon so overcome with joy that he cried out, 'Tis enough; 'tis enough; mine eyes have beheld; mine eyes have beheld."

When Joseph returned to the Whitmer home, he sat down by his mother. So much had happened to the young prophet in the past decade, though he was not yet twenty-four years old. He exclaimed to his mother and father: "Father, mother, you do not know how happy I am: the Lord has now caused the plates to be shown to three more besides myself. . . . and they will have to bear witness to the truth of what I have said . . . and I feel as if I was relieved of a burden which was almost too heavy for me to bear."[5]

A short time after the Three Witnesses saw the plates, Joseph, with Christian, Jacob, Peter, and John Whitmer, and their brother-in-law Hiram Page, visited the Smiths in Manchester. The Prophet invited his father and brothers, Hyrum and Samuel, to join them. They retired to the woods near the Smith residence, and there . . . Joseph took the plates from the cloth container and laid them before the eyes of the eight men. There was no blaze of celestial light to illumine the forest about them, no angel awed them with his presence, and no divine voice from the heavens pierced them to the marrow. One mortal man placed into the hands of eight other mortal men a heavy gold book of great antiquity and said, in effect: "Gentlemen, here are the plates of the Nephite history, which the angel entrusted to me, from which I translated by the power of God the Book of Mormon manuscript into English."

Each of the eight men, from fifty-eight-year-old Joseph Smith, Sr., to Peter Whitmer, Jr., a youth of nineteen years, handled the plates, hefted them, and examined the ancient engravings.

In the evening at the Smith home the Eight Witnesses bore [the testimony found in the introduction to the Book of Mormon].[6]

Testimonies of the eleven special witnesses to the Book of Mormon

Critics of the Church have over the years tried to discount the testimonies of the eleven special witnesses who saw (and eight of them handled) the plates. However, "from the time the eleven witnesses were shown the plates in June, 1829, to the day they died, they upheld their undeviating testimony to friend and foe alike."[7] Most of the witnesses had their personal testimonies recorded so as to leave no doubt about their witness.

Of the eleven, four (three Whitmer sons, David, John, and Jacob, and their brother-in-law, Hiram Page) died outside of The Church of Jesus Christ of Latter-day Saints, but remained true to their testimonies. The three Smiths died from exposure, exhaustion, and persecution as martyrs to the cause. Oliver Cowdery and Martin Harris spent some time outside of the Church, but returned before their deaths to full fellowship. Examples of some of their testimonies follow.

On September 7, 1878, in a conversation with Elders Orson Pratt and Joseph F. Smith, David Whitmer said:

Joseph, Oliver, and myself were together when I saw them [the plates]. We not only saw the plates of the Book of Mormon, but also the brass plates, the plates of the Book of Ether . . . and many other plates. . . . the sword of Laban, the Directors [the Liahona Lehi had], and the Interpreters [Urim and Thummim]. I saw them just as plain as I see this bed (striking the bed beside him with his hand), and I heard the voice of the Lord, as distinctly as I ever heard anything in my life, declaring that the records of the plates of the Book of Mormon were translated by the gift and power of God.[8]

Martin Harris, before he returned to fellowship in the Church, was asked if he actually believed he had seen an angel. He replied: "Gentlemen, what I have said is true, from the fact that my belief is swallowed up in knowledge; for I want to say to you that as the Lord lives I do know that I stood with the Prophet Joseph Smith in the presence of the angel, and it was in the brightness of day."[9]

In returning to the Church, Oliver Cowdery arrived with his wife and daughter at the eastern headquarters of the Church in Kanesville, Iowa. On October 21, 1848, he addressed the Saints and testified that he wrote with his own pen, except for a few pages, the entire Book of Mormon as the Prophet Joseph Smith "translated it by the gift and power of God, by the means of the Urim and Thummim." He further witnessed: "I beheld with my eyes, and handled with my hands, the gold plates. . . . I also saw with my eyes and handled with my hands the 'holy interpreters.' That book is *true*. . . . It contains the principles of salvation; and if you, my hearers, will walk by its light and obey its precepts, you will be saved with an everlasting salvation in the kingdom of God on high."[10]

John Whitmer, who was excommunicated for "persisting in un-Christian-like conduct," never rejoined the Church. Once, however, when asked by Theodore Turley, in the presence of hostile Missourians, if he denied his testimony "that an angel did present those plates to Joseph Smith," he said: "I now say, I handled those plates; there were fine engravings on both sides. I handled them; they were shown to me by a supernatural power."[11]

What happened to the plates after the translation was completed

The actual translation of the Book of Mormon record was accomplished in the relatively short period of about seventy-five working days.[12] Joseph said: "They [the plates] remained safe in my hands, until I had accomplished by them what was required at my hand. When, according to arrangements, the messenger called for them, I delivered them up to him; and he has them in his charge until this day."[13]

Brigham Young gave the following account regarding the return of the plates:

> The angel instructed [Joseph] to carry them [the plates] back to the hill Cumorah, which he did. Oliver says that when Joseph and Oliver went there, the hill opened, and they walked into a cave, in which there was a large and spacious room. He says he did not think, at the time, whether they had the light of the sun, or artificial light; but that it was just as light as day.
>
> They laid the plates on a table . . . that stood in the room. Under this table there was a pile of plates as much as two feet high, and there were altogether in this room more plates than probably many wagon loads; they were piled up in the corners and along the walls.[14]

Mormon makes it clear that he hid in the Hill Cumorah many plates. "I . . . hid up in the hill Cumorah all the records which had been entrusted to me by the hand of the Lord, save it were these few plates which I gave unto my son Moroni" (Mormon 6:6).

At one point in time, when the persecution was particularly severe, an angel took the plates from Harmony, Pennsylvania, to Fayette, New York, for Joseph so that he and Oliver could continue the work of translation there. David Whitmer reported as follows:

> When I was returning to Fayette with Joseph and Oliver . . . a very pleasant, nice-looking old man suddenly appeared by the side of our wagon and saluted us with "Good morning, it is very warm."
>
> . . . . I invited him to ride if he was going our way, but he said very pleasantly, "No, I am going to Cumorah." This was something new to me, I did not know what Cumorah meant, and as I looked inquiringly of Joseph, the old man instantly disappeared, so that I did not see him again.

David observed the appearance of the stranger. He was a little above the average in height for a man, rather heavyset, with a large face and white hair and beard. He wore a brown woolen suit and carried a knapsack on his back containing an object shaped like a book. David learned from the Prophet that he was the angelic messenger who had taken the plates prior to their departure from Harmony to Fayette.[15]

Joseph knew how to recognize angels. Most of us do not. Paul reminds us all in his writings to the Hebrews, "Be not forgetful to entertain strangers: for thereby some have entertained angels unawares" (Hebrews 13:2).

"The most correct of any book on earth"

Many people have asked, how could Joseph Smith possibly say that the Book of Mormon is the most correct of any book on earth? Doesn't this show a lack of humility? And what about the Bible, which even Latter-day Saints accept as the first witness of Jesus Christ?

Joseph Smith's words were: "I told the brethren that the Book of Mormon was the most correct of any book on earth, and the keystone of our religion, and a man would get nearer to God by abiding by its precepts, than by any other book."[16]

No lack of humility was involved in his statement. The Book of Mormon is a unique volume of scripture. With its publication, for the first time in history a book of scripture was available to the world which had been:

> Written by prophets (Ether through Moroni)
> Edited by prophets (Mormon and Moroni)
> Translated by a prophet (Joseph Smith)

Even the Bible, as valuable and beautiful as it is, cannot claim to have been edited and translated by a living prophet who had the power and the right to commune with the heavens. No other scripture has been translated by a prophet into a modern language. Men of good faith have done their best to translate the Bible, but many other men have tried to improve upon their work. What indeed is the true word of God?

In the eighth Article of Faith, the Prophet Joseph Smith stated: "We believe the Bible to be the word of God as far as it is translated correctly." But speaking of the Book of Mormon, he added, "we also believe the Book of Mormon to be the word of God."

The Lord Jesus Christ confirmed Joseph's work when he spoke to the Three Witnesses in June 1829: "He [Joseph Smith] has translated the book, even that part which I have commanded him, and as your Lord and your God liveth it is true" (D&C 17:6). In March 1830, the Lord told Martin Harris: "Impart . . . freely to the printing of the Book of Mormon, which contains the truth and the word of God" (D&C 19:26).

On the day the Church was organized, the Lord said: "[God] gave him power from on high, by the means which were before prepared, to translate the Book of Mormon. . . . And those who receive it in faith, and work righteousness, shall receive a crown of eternal life; but those who harden their hearts in unbelief, and reject it, it shall turn to their own condemnation." (D&C 20:8, 14–15.)

Today, millions of believers, members of The Church of Jesus Christ of Latter-day Saints, and even some nonmembers, accept the Book of Mormon as the word of God. It is probably "more widely read than any other volume save the Bible."[17] Its impact on the Christian world continues to grow daily, and every year hundreds of thousands accept its message.

Why Joseph didn't show the plates to more people

Joseph's younger brother William, although he did not move west to be with the main body of the Saints, never lost his testimony of his brother Joseph, nor that of the translation of the gold plates into the Book of Mormon. One day about two weeks before his death, he responded to an interviewer's questions about the gold plates.

The interviewer asked, "if he [William] ever saw the plates his brother had had, from which the Book of Mormon was translated." William answered: "I did not see them uncovered, but I handled them and hefted them while wrapped in a tow frock and judged them to have weighed about sixty pounds. I could tell they were plates of some kind and that they were fastened together by rings running through the back. Their size was as described in mother's history."

The interviewer asked, "Did any others of the family see them?"

"Yes," said he, "father and my brother Samuel saw them as I did while in the frock. So did Hyrum and others of the family." . . .

"Didn't you want to remove the cloth and see the bare plates?"

"No," he replied; "for father had just asked if he might not be permitted to do so, and Joseph, putting his hand on them said, 'No, I am instructed not to show them to any one. If I do, I will transgress and lose them again.' Besides we did not care to have him break the commandment and suffer as he did before."

"Did you not doubt Joseph's testimony sometimes?"

"No," was the reply. "We all had the most implicit confidence in what he said. He was a truthful boy. Father and mother believed him, why should not the children? I suppose if he had told crooked stories about other things we might have doubted his word about the plates, but Joseph was a truthful boy. That father and mother believed his report and suffered persecution for that belief shows that he was truthful. No sir, we never doubted his word for one minute."[18]

The challenge of duplication

If a person scoffs at the missionary's explanation of the Book of Mormon, he is in so many words claiming it to be false; a deceiving fraud formulated through the efforts and talents of a common man—Joseph Smith, Jr. History has shown that what is produced by one man can be duplicated by another man, and most often made even better. The challenge the Book of Mormon makes to the world is that of duplication. In order to meet the challenge, one must produce a comparable record while complying with the same conditions experienced by the original author.

Here is the challenge.

1. Write the history of an ancient land like Tibet. Why Tibet, you ask? Because you know more about Tibet than the young Joseph Smith knew about ancient America before he met Moroni. But if you don't like Tibet, pick some other ancient culture.

"The Angel Moroni Appears to Joseph in His Room," by Tom Lovell.
Used by permission of The Church of Jesus Christ of Latter-day Saints.

2

Charity

If a man be meek and lowly in heart, and confesses by the power of the Holy Ghost that Jesus is the Christ, he must needs have charity; for if he have not charity he is nothing. . . .

Charity is the pure love of Christ, and it endureth forever; and whoso is found possessed of it at the last day, it shall be well with him. . . .

. . . When [Jesus Christ] shall appear we shall be like him, for we shall see him as he is; that we may have this hope; that we may be purified even as he is pure. Amen.
—Moroni 7:44, 47–48

"I feel sorry for this brother to the amount of five dollars"

When the Saints had been driven from Missouri and began to settle in Illinois, Joseph went to Quincy, where "he visited around from house to house among the Saints to see how they were situated, and gave words of strength and encouragement to them." When informed some time later that a brother who lived some distance from Nauvoo had had his house burned down, nearly everyone present expressed sympathy for the man. But Joseph put his hand in his pocket, took out five dollars, and said: "I feel sorry for this brother to the amount of five dollars; how much do you feel sorry?"[1]

"In less than two hours my wife loved him better than she did me"

Joseph not only gave charity to others but also received it from members of the Church as well as nonmembers who

17

could not stand to see the "Mormons" treated so badly. One such example of unsolicited charity and friendship came from the wife of General Moses Wilson, a self-proclaimed "Mormon" hater who was instructed to take Joseph Smith to Jackson County, Missouri, after he had narrowly escaped being put to death. General Wilson, speaking about the Prophet, said: "He was a very remarkable man. I carried him into my house, a prisoner in chains, and in less than two hours my wife loved him better than she did me."[2]

Although Mrs. Wilson never joined the Church, she continued to show love and charity towards the small group of people who followed their beloved Prophet so faithfully. George A. Smith tells the following story:

> Mrs. Wilson became deeply interested in preserving the life of Joseph Smith and the other prisoners, and this interest on her part, which probably arose from a spirit of humanity, did not end with that circumstance, for, a number of years afterwards, after the family had moved to Texas, General Wilson became interested in raising a mob to do violence to some of the Latter-day Saint Elders who were going to preach in the neighborhood, and this coming to the ears of Mrs. Wilson, although then an aged lady, she mounted her horse and rode thirty miles to give the Elders the information. . . .[Years later] . . . a son of Mr. Wilson . . . told me that his mother deeply deprecated the difficulties with the Mormons, and did all she could to prevent them.[3]

"He can never eat without his friends"

Under the date of Thursday, January 4, 1844, Joseph gives us a little glimpse into his and Emma's love for their family and friends:

> I took dinner in the north room, and was remarking to Brother Phelps what a kind, provident wife I had,—that when I wanted a little bread and milk, she would load the table with so many good things it would destroy my appetite.
> At this moment Emma came in, while Phelps, in continuation of the conversation said, "You must do as Bonaparte

did—have a little table, just large enough for victuals you want yourself."

Mrs. Smith replied, "Mr. Smith is a bigger man than Bonaparte. He can never eat without his friends."

I remarked, "That is the wisest thing I ever heard you say."[4]

Joseph's great promise to women: "The angels cannot be restrained from being your associates"

On March 17, 1842, Joseph organized the women of the Church into the Female Relief Society of Nauvoo. In the upper room of the Red Brick Store, Joseph had made a large meeting room called the Lodge Room. Here the ladies were blessed, and Emma, Joseph's wife, was called to be the first president of the society.

Later Joseph admonished the sisters to do charitable works, that they might provoke the brethren to good works in looking to the wants of the poor—searching after objects of charity, and administering to their wants—assist by correcting the morals and strengthening the virtues of the community.[5]

On April 28, 1842, Joseph again went to their meeting. Bathsheba Smith recollected that the Prophet opened the meeting with prayer. She remembered that during the prayer "his voice trembled very much." In his remarks he said, "According to my prayer I will not be with you long to teach and instruct you; and the world will not be troubled with me much longer."[6]

Joseph then bestowed upon the sisters the following promise:

It is natural for females to have feelings of charity and benevolence. You are now placed in a situation in which you can act according to those sympathies which God has planted in your bosoms.

If you live up to these principles, how great and glorious will be your reward in the celestial kingdom! If you live up to your privileges, the angels cannot be restrained from being your associates.[7]

"I am sorry, Anthony, but the law must be observed"

While [the Prophet was] acting as mayor of the city [Nauvoo], a colored man called Anthony was arrested for selling liquor on Sunday, contrary to law. He pleaded that the reason he had done so was that he might raise the money to purchase the freedom of a dear child held as a slave in a Southern state. He had been able to purchase the liberty of himself and wife and now wished to bring his little child to their new home.

[Joseph said,] "I am sorry, Anthony, but the law must be observed, and we will have to impose a fine."

The next day Brother Joseph presented Anthony with a fine horse, directing him to sell it, and use the money obtained for the purchase of the child.[8]

Joseph was never too busy to show charity

Charles Dana tells how the Prophet Joseph took time from his busy schedule to bring comfort to a desperate friend.

Charles Dana wrote that his wife became so ill in Nauvoo that he despaired of her life. In desperation, he "mustered courage to go for Joseph."

He found the Prophet very busy and concerned over an important document that had been lost. As Joseph left the house with several others to go in search of the missing item, Dana took the opportunity, "as he was passing out of the gate," to say, "Bro. Joseph will you go and administer to my wife?" The hasty answer was, "I cannot!" But, with tears in his eyes, Charles pleaded, "Bro. Joseph she is sick nigh unto death; and I do not want to part with her."

Charles's description continues: "He turned his head, saw my countenance and answered. 'I will be there presently.' My heart leaped for joy; I hurried home. . . . I had not much more than got there before Bro. Joseph came bounding over the bottom like a chased Roe. He asked me, 'How long has she been so sick?' He then walked the house for some minutes; I began to fear that he considered her past recovery; but he finally went to the fire, warmed his hands, throwed his cloak off, went to the bed, laid his hands upon her . . . and pronounced great blessings upon her."[9]

The charitable in Illinois

After his escape from Liberty Jail, Joseph finally arrived in Quincy, Illinois, on April 22, 1839, "amidst the congratulations of my friends, and the embraces of my family, whom I found as well as could be expected, considering what they had been called to endure."[10]

The Saints had been warmly received in Quincy following their expulsion from Missouri. The citizens of that community, and especially a group known as the Democratic Association, had met there the previous February to consider the plight of the exiles and the ways which they might be assisted. Out of that meeting came a resolution: "Resolved, That the strangers recently arrived here from the state of Missouri, known by the name of the 'Latter-day Saints,' are entitled to our sympathy and kindest regard, and that we recommend to the citizens of Quincy to extend all the kindness in their power to bestow on the persons who are in affliction."[11]

Charity works both ways

Joseph loved the parable of the Savior's as recorded in Matthew, which is the scriptural basis for the great hymn "A Poor Wayfaring Man of Grief."

Then shall the King say unto them on his right hand, Come, ye blessed of my Father, inherit the kingdom prepared for you from the foundation of the world:

For I was an hungred, and ye gave me meat: I was thirsty, and ye gave me drink: I was a stranger, and ye took me in:

Naked, and ye clothed me: I was sick, and ye visited me: I was in prison, and ye came unto me.

Then shall the righteous answer him, saying, Lord, when saw we thee an hungred, and fed thee? or thirsty, and gave thee drink?

When saw we thee a stranger, and took thee in? or naked, and clothed thee?

Or when saw we thee sick, or in prison, and came unto thee?

And the King shall answer and say unto them, Verily I say unto you, Inasmuch as ye have done it unto one of the least of these my brethren, ye have done it unto me. (Matthew 25:34–40.)

Joseph was not only charitable but also was the recipient of charity. In his sixteen years of marriage, he and Emma never really had much peace. They moved at least twelve times; and six children, his father, and two brothers preceded him in death. Many Saints were willing to give their best to the Prophet of God. May their glory be assured when they meet him in the kingdoms on high.

"Come, ye blessed of my Father."

3

Courage

Brethren, shall we not go on in so great a cause? Go forward and not backward. Courage, brethren; and on, on to the victory! Let your hearts rejoice, and be exceedingly glad.

—D&C 128:22

One of the most daring and heroic deeds

Joseph Smith recorded:

While on the mountains some distance from Washington, our coachman stepped into a public house to take his grog [a drink of rum], when the horses took fright and ran down the hill at full speed. I persuaded my fellow travelers to be quiet and retain their seats, but had to hold one woman to prevent her throwing her infant out of the coach.

The passengers were exceedingly agitated, but I used every persuasion to calm their feelings; and opening the door, I secured my hold on the side of the coach the best way I could, and succeeded in placing myself in the coachman's seat, and reining up the horses, after they had run some two or three miles, and neither coach, horses, or passengers received any injury.

My course was spoken of in the highest terms of commendation, as being one of the most daring and heroic deeds, and no language could express the gratitude of the passengers, when they found themselves safe, and the horses quiet. There were some members of Congress with us, who proposed naming the incident to that body, believing they would reward such conduct by some public act; but on inquiring my name, to mention as the author of their safety, and finding it to be Joseph Smith, the "Mormon Prophet," as they called me, I heard no more of their praise, gratitude, or reward.[1]

"Judge ye for yourselves"

And as for perils which I am called to pass through, they seem but a small thing to me, as the envy and wrath of man have been my common lot all the days of my life; and for what cause it seems mysterious, unless I was ordained from before the foundation of the world for some good end, or bad, as you may choose to call it. Judge ye for yourselves. God knoweth all these things whether it be good or bad. But nevertheless, deep water is what I am wont to swim in. It all has become a second nature to me; and I feel, like Paul, to glory in tribulation; for to this day has the God of my fathers delivered me out of them all, and will deliver me from henceforth; for behold, and lo, I shall triumph over all my enemies, for the Lord God hath spoken it. (D&C 127:2.)

"Majesty have I seen but once"

Parley P. Pratt recorded the following in his autobiography:

In one of those tedious nights we had lain as if in sleep till the hour of midnight had passed, and our ears and hearts had been pained, while we had listened for hours to the obscene jests, the horrid oaths, the dreadful blasphemies and filthy language of our guards . . . as they recounted to each other their deeds of rapine, murder, robbery, etc, which they had committed among the "Mormons" while at Far West and vicinity. They even boasted of defiling by force wives, daughters, and virgins, and of shooting or dashing out the brains of men, women and children.

I had listened till I became so disgusted, shocked, horrified, and so filled with the spirit of indignant justice that I could scarcely refrain from rising upon my feet and rebuking the guards; but had said nothing to Joseph, or anyone else, although I lay next to him and knew he was awake.

On a sudden he arose to his feet, and spoke in a voice of thunder, or as the roaring lion, uttering, as near as I can recollect, the following words:

"*Silence*, ye fiends of the infernal pit! In the name of Jesus Christ I rebuke you, and command you to be still; I will not live another minute and hear such language. Cease such talk, or you or I die *this instant!*"

He ceased to speak. He stood erect in terrible majesty. Chained, and without a weapon; calm, unruffled and dignified as an angel, he looked upon the quailing guards, whose weapons were lowered or dropped to the ground; whose knees smote together, and who, shrinking into a corner, or crouching at his feet, begged his pardon, and remained quiet till a change of guards.

I have seen the ministers of justice, clothed in magisterial robes, and criminals arraigned before them, while life was suspended on a breath, in the Courts of England; I have witnessed a Congress in solemn session to give laws to nations; I have tried to conceive of kings, of royal courts, of thrones and crowns, and of emperors assembled to decide the fate of kingdoms; but dignity and majesty have I seen but *once*, as it stood in chains, at midnight, in a dungeon in an obscure village of Missouri.[2]

"It is cold-blooded murder"

Destruction came at Far West, and the Prophet was betrayed into the hands of his enemies by Colonel George Hinkle, a trusted associate. Joseph was one of the several Church leaders to be so betrayed. Parley Pratt wrote of that first abusive night when he, Joseph Smith, and others were prisoners:

We were placed under a strong guard, and were without shelter during the night, lying on the ground in the open air, in the midst of a great rain. The guards during the whole night kept up a constant tirade of mockery, and the most obscene blackguardism and abuse. They blasphemed God; mocked Jesus Christ; swore the most dreadful oaths; taunted Brother Joseph and others; demanded miracles; wanted signs, such as "Come Mr. Smith, show us an angel." "Give us one of your revelations." "Show us a miracle."

"Come, there is one of your brethren here in camp whom
we took prisoner yesterday in his own house, and knocked
his brains out with his own rifle, which we found over his
fireplace; he lays speechless and dying; speak the word and
heal him, and then we will all believe." "Or, if you are
Apostles or men of God, deliver yourselves, and then we will
be Mormons."

Next would be a volley of oaths and blasphemies; then a
tumultuous tirade of lewd boastings of having defiled virgins and wives by force, etc., much of which I dare not
write, and, indeed, language would fail me to attempt more
than a faint description.

Thus passed this dreadful night, and before morning
several other captives were added to our number.[3]

The Prophet's life was spared only by the courageous act of
Alexander Doniphan. Brigadier-General Doniphan received an
illegal order from his commanding officer, Major-General
Samuel Lucas: "Brigadier-General Doniphan: Sir:—You will take
Joseph Smith and the other prisoners into the public square of
Far West, and shoot them at 9 o'clock tomorrow morning."

General Doniphan wasted no time in sending a bold reply
to his superior officer: "It is cold-blooded murder. I will not
obey your order. My brigade shall march for Liberty tomorrow
morning, at 8 o'clock; and if you execute these men, I will hold
you responsible before an earthly tribunal, so help me God."[4]

The prisoners somehow heard of the order, and kneeled
in prayer, and prayed fervently that it might not be executed. And it was not. Flagrantly insubordinate as was
General Doniphan's refusal, he was never called to account
for it.

The Mormons have always remembered General Doniphan's humanity on this occasion as well as others, and
when, in 1873, he went to Salt Lake City, he was received
with much feeling, and shown every regard and attention
by Brigham Young and other authorities of the church and
city, and by even the masses of the people.[5]

"Joseph arose like a lion about to roar"

Again, from Parley P. Pratt's autobiography:

While visiting with Brother Joseph in Philadelphia, a very large church was opened for him to preach in, and about three thousand people assembled to hear him. Brother Rigdon spoke first, and dwelt on the Gospel, illustrating his doctrine by the Bible.

When he was through, Brother Joseph arose like a lion about to roar; and being full of the Holy Ghost, spoke in great power, bearing testimony of the visions he had seen, the ministering of angels which he had enjoyed; and how he had found the plates of the Book of Mormon, and translated them by the gift and power of God.

He commenced by saying: "If nobody else had the courage to testify of so glorious a message from Heaven and of the finding of so glorious a record, he felt to do it in justice to the people, and leave the event with God."

The entire congregation were astounded; electrified, as it were, and overwhelmed with the sense of the truth and power by which he spoke, and the wonders which he related. A lasting impression was made; many souls were gathered into the fold. And I bear witness, that he, by his faithful and powerful testimony, cleared his garments of their blood![6]

"Thinking that it would save the lives of his brethren"

Elder John Taylor wrote of the martyrdom of Joseph Smith as follows (see D&C 135:4–5):

When Joseph went to Carthage to deliver himself up to the pretended requirements of the law, two or three days previous to his assassination, he said: "I am going like a lamb to the slaughter; but I am calm as a summer's morning; I have a conscience void of offense towards God, and towards all men. I shall die innocent, and it shall yet be said of me—he was murdered in cold blood."

The same morning, after Hyrum had made ready to go—shall it be said to the slaughter? yes, for so it was—he read the following paragraph, near the close of the twelfth chapter of Ether, in the Book of Mormon, and turned down the leaf upon it. . . .

"And now I . . . bid farewell unto the Gentiles; yea, and also unto my brethren whom I love, until we shall meet before the judgment-seat of Christ, where all men shall know that my garments are not spotted with your blood."

A few excerpts from the Church history statement of the martyrdom of Joseph and Hyrum help us see the courage of Joseph right to the end of his mortal life. He knew he had to die, for it had been ordained in the heavens long before his birth. Yet he thought of his friends and their safety first.

Carthage Jail, June 27, 1844

Immediately there was a little rustling at the outer door of the jail . . . and also a discharge of three or four firearms followed instantly. The doctor glanced an eye by the curtain of the window, and saw about a hundred armed men around the door.

. . . The mob encircled the building, and some of them rushed by the guard up the flight of stairs, burst open the door, and began the work of death, while others fired in through the open windows.

In the meantime Joseph, Hyrum, and Elder Taylor had their coats off. Joseph sprang to his coat for his six-shooter, Hyrum for his single barrel, Taylor for Markham's large hickory cane, and Dr. Richards for Taylor's cane. All sprang against the door, the balls whistled up the stairway, and in an instant one came through the door.

Joseph Smith, John Taylor and Dr. Richards sprang to the left of the door, and tried to knock aside the guns of the ruffians.

Hyrum was retreating back in front of the door and snapped his pistol, when a ball struck him in the left side of his nose, and he fell on his back on the floor saying, "I am a dead man!" . . .

When Hyrum fell, Joseph exclaimed, "Oh dear, brother Hyrum!" and opening the door a few inches he discharged his six shooter in the stairway. . . .

Joseph, seeing there was no safety in the room, and no doubt thinking that it would save the lives of his brethren in the room if he could get out, turned calmly from the door, dropped his pistol on the floor, and sprang into the window when two balls pierced him from the door, and one entered his right breast from without, and he fell outward into the hands of his murderers, exclaiming, "O Lord, my God!"[7]

In these few seconds, Joseph proved again his courage and his willingness to follow his friend and elder brother, Jesus Christ, the Savior of all mankind, who declared: "Greater love hath no man than this, that a man lay down his life for his friends" (John 15:13).

The courage of Oliver Cowdery

After Oliver Cowdery had been excommunicated from the Church, he moved to Elkhorn, Wisconsin, and took up the practice of law. Later he moved to Michigan, where he was elected prosecuting attorney. The defending attorney in a murder case sarcastically asked him, in court, to "tell us something about that golden Bible that Joe Smith dug out of the hill." Under that pressure, Oliver still did not deny his testimony. With great courage he rose and made the following comments:

May it please the court and gentlemen of the jury, my brother attorney on the other side has charged me with connection with Joseph Smith and the golden Bible. The responsibility has been placed upon me, and I cannot escape reply.

Before God and man I dare not deny what I have said, and what my testimony contains as written and printed on the front page of the Book of Mormon. May it please your honor and gentlemen of the jury, this I say:

I saw the angel and heard his voice—how can I deny it? It happened in the daytime when the sun was shining bright in the firmament; not in the night when I was asleep. That glorious messenger from heaven, dressed in white, standing above the ground, in a glory I have never seen anything to compare with—the sun insignificant in comparison—told us if we denied that testimony there is no forgiveness in this life or in the world to come. Now how can I deny it—I dare not: I will not![8]

"Take the oath or you'll never leave here alive"

One of the greatest stories of courage in Church history is that of Dennison Harris and Robert Scott. The Prophet had been informed that there was a traitor in the Church in Nauvoo who was conspiring to deliver him to the Missourians. Dennison Harris and Robert Scott, two young men, approached Joseph in March 1844 and told him that they had been invited to the secret meetings that would discuss what to do with Joseph Smith. They asked Joseph whether they should attend.

Joseph suggested that they do so, and then report to him, but to be sure not to agree to participate in the conspirators' plans. Twice they attended meetings and then went to the riverbank to report to Joseph.

After two meetings, Joseph knew the young men were in danger of being exposed as his supporters and losing their lives. The group was about to take secret oaths to take his life. He told Dennison and Robert: "This will be the last time they will admit you to their councils. They will come to some determination, but be sure that you make no covenant, nor enter into any obligations with them. They may threaten your lives if you do not, but be brave."

Arriving at William Law's house, they were alarmed to find two men with muskets guarding the door. Francis Higbee sat at a table and exacted from each entrant an oath: "You solemnly swear, before God and all holy angels, and those your brethren by whom you are surrounded, that you will give your life, your liberty, your influence, your all, for the destruction of Joseph Smith, so help you God.'"

Each person sworn placed his hand on a Bible and signed his name.

After each had taken the oath . . . Harris and Scott were asked to take the oath. They refused. . . . They started to leave but were stopped by the guard: "You're not leaving without taking the oath." They were told, "You know all our plans and we don't propose that you leave in that style. You either take the oath or you'll never leave here alive."

Surrounded by men with knives and swords, the boys saw no chance to escape; yet they were resolute. The Laws and the Higbees would have shed the boys' blood if one of the group had not reminded them that the boys' parents knew of their presence at the meetings; if they did not return home, a search would be made. This reminder intimidated the leaders, and after threatening the youths that they would be killed if they ever divulged what they had heard and seen, they let the boys go.

Hurrying to the river bank, they met the Prophet and told their story. Tears flowed freely from the Prophet's eyes at the recital, and he exacted a promise from the boys never to tell their experience to anyone for twenty years.[9]

Courage to save the scriptures

Nephi showed great courage and put his life in danger to return to Jerusalem to acquire the brass plates because "they were desirable; yea, even of great worth unto us, insomuch that we could preserve the commandments of the Lord unto our children" (1 Nephi 5:21). Likewise, some of the Saints showed great courage in protecting the Book of Commandments, the book that was the beginning of what today we call the Doctrine and Covenants.

In Missouri, W. W. Phelps began printing copies of this book for the Saints. While the printing was taking place, an enraged mob entered the house, threw his furniture and the printing press out of the window, destroyed the type, and burned most of the written revelations. They tore down the brick structure, covering the two Phelps children, Henry and his younger brother, with broken bricks and debris. Fortunately, they were not injured.[10]

Many of the printed sheets of the *Book of Commandments* were carried and dumped in an old log stable nearby. John Taylor [who had observed the destruction of the press] asked Bishop Partridge if he might step into the stable and retrieve some copies of the *Book of Commandments*. The bishop cautioned him that such an attempt would "most likely cost [him his] life." Young Taylor replied that he "did not mind hazarding [his] life to secure some of the printed copies of the commandments." Impressed with his courage,

the bishop granted him permission to try. John Taylor reported:

"I ran my hand into a crack between the logs, and
pulled out a few at a time until I got as many as I could
carry. When I was discovered a dozen men surrounded me
and commenced throwing stones at me, and I shouted out,
"Oh My God must I be stoned to death like Stephen for the
sake of the word of the Lord?" The Lord gave me strength
and skill to elude them and make my escape without being
hit by a stone. I delivered the copies to Bishop Partridge,
who said that I had done a good work and my escape was a
miracle. These I believe are the only copies of that edition of
the *Book of Commandments* preserved from destruction.[11]

He was unaware, however, that through the courage of two
young girls, several other sheets were saved before the mob
threw the copies into the heap in the old log stable.

Mary Elizabeth Rollins and her sister hid behind a rail
fence and watched the members of the mob carry copies of
the *Book of Commandments* out of the printing office and
throw them into a pile, intending to burn them. The
teenage girls were determined to save some of the books.
"They will kill us [if they see us]," said Mary's sister. But
both agreed to risk it. . . . the girls rushed out, filled their
aprons with the books, and fled to a corn field nearby.
Some of the mob saw them and yelled for them to halt.
Mary Elizabeth recalled:

"But we ran as fast as we could. Two of them started
after us. Seeing a gap in a fence, we entered into a large
cornfield, laid the papers on the ground, and hid them with
our persons. The corn was from five to six feet high, and
very thick; they hunted around considerable, and came
very near us but did not find us."[12]

4

Death and Funeral Messages

And I soon go to the place of my rest, which is with my Redeemer; for I know that in him I shall rest. And I rejoice in the day when my mortal shall put on immortality, and shall stand before him; then shall I see his face with pleasure, and he will say unto me: Come unto me, ye blessed, there is a place prepared for you in the mansions of my Father.

—Enos 1:27

Martyrdom of Joseph Smith the Prophet and his brother Hyrum

To seal the testimony of this book and the Book of Mormon, we announce the martyrdom of Joseph Smith the Prophet, and Hyrum Smith the Patriarch. They were shot in Carthage jail, on the 27th of June, 1844, about five o'clock P.M., by an armed mob —painted black—of from 150 to 200 persons. Hyrum was shot first and fell calmly, exclaiming: *I am a dead man!* Joseph leaped from the window, and was shot dead in the attempt, exclaiming: *O Lord my God!* They were both shot after they were dead, in a brutal manner, and both received four balls.

John Taylor and Willard Richards, two of the Twelve, were the only persons in the room at the time; the former was wounded in a savage manner with four balls, but has since recovered; the latter, through the providence of God, escaped, without even a hole in his robe.

Joseph Smith, the Prophet and Seer of the Lord, has done more, save Jesus only, for the salvation of men in this world, than any other man that ever lived in it. In the short space of twenty years, he has brought forth the Book of

Mormon, which he translated by the gift and power of God, and has been the means of publishing it on two continents; has sent the fulness of the everlasting gospel, which it contained, to the four quarters of the earth; has brought forth the revelations and commandments which compose this book of Doctrine and Covenants, and many other wise documents and instructions for the benefit of the children of men; gathered many thousands of the Latter-day Saints, founded a great city, and left a fame and name that cannot be slain. He lived great, and he died great in the eyes of God and his people; and like most of the Lord's anointed in ancient times, has sealed his mission and his works with his own blood; and so has his brother Hyrum. In life they were not divided, and in death they were not separated!

When Joseph went to Carthage to deliver himself up to the pretended requirements of the law, two or three days previous to his assassination, he said: "I am going like a lamb to the slaughter; but I am calm as a summer's morning; I have a conscience void of offense towards God, and towards all men. I shall die innocent, and it shall yet be said of me—he was murdered in cold blood."

The same morning, after Hyrum had made ready to go—shall it be said to the slaughter? yes, for so it was—he read the following paragraph, near the close of the twelfth chapter of Ether, in the Book of Mormon, and turned down the leaf upon it:

"And it came to pass that I prayed unto the Lord that he would give unto the Gentiles grace, that they might have charity. And it came to pass that the Lord said unto me: If they have not charity it mattereth not unto thee, thou hast been faithful; wherefore thy garments shall be made clean. And because thou hast seen thy weakness, thou shalt be made strong, even unto the sitting down in the place which I have prepared in the mansions of my Father. And now I . . . bid farewell unto the Gentiles; yea, and also unto my brethren whom I love, until we shall meet before the judgment-seat of Christ, where all men shall know that my garments are not spotted with your blood." The testators are now dead, and their testament is in force.

Hyrum Smith was forty-four years old in February, 1844, and Joseph Smith was thirty-eight in December, 1843; and henceforward their names will be classed among the martyrs of religion; and the reader in every nation will be reminded that the Book of Mormon, and this book of Doctrine and Covenants of the church, cost the best blood of the nineteenth century to bring them forth for the salvation of a ruined world; and that if the fire can scathe a green tree for the glory of God, how easy it will burn up the dry trees to purify the vineyard of corruption. They lived for glory; they died for glory; and glory is their eternal reward. From age to age shall their names go down to posterity as gems for the sanctified.

They were innocent of any crime, as they had often been proved before, and were only confined in the jail by the conspiracy of traitors and wicked men; and their *innocent blood* on the floor of Carthage jail is a broad seal affixed to "Mormonism" that cannot be rejected by any court on earth, and their *innocent blood* on the escutcheon of the State of Illinois, with the broken faith of the State as pledged by the governor, is a witness to the truth of the everlasting gospel that all the world cannot impeach; and their *innocent blood* on the banner of liberty, and on the *magna charta* of the United States, is an ambassador for the religion of Jesus Christ, that will touch the hearts of honest men among all nations; and their *innocent blood* with the innocent blood of all the martyrs under the altar that John saw, will cry unto the Lord of Hosts till he avenges that blood on the earth, Amen. (D&C 135.)

Two minutes in the Carthage Jail

The following is copied from a *Times and Seasons* article written by Willard Richards:

Possibly the following events occupied near three minutes, but I think only about two, and have penned them for the gratification of many friends.

Carthage, June 27, 1844.

A shower of musket balls were thrown up the stairway against the door of the prison in the second story, followed by many rapid footsteps.

While Generals Joseph and Hyrum Smith, Mr. Taylor,

and myself, who were in the front chamber, closed the door of our room against the entry at the head of the stairs, and placed ourselves against it, there being no lock on the door, and no catch that was usable.

The door is a common panel, and as soon as we heard the feet at the stairs head, a ball was sent through the door, which passed between us, and showed that our enemies were desperadoes, and we must change our position.

General Joseph Smith, Mr. Taylor and myself sprang back to the front part of the room, and General Hyrum Smith retreated two-thirds across the chamber directly in front of and facing the door.

A ball was sent through the door which hit Hyrum on the side of his nose, when he fell backwards, extended at length, without moving his feet.

From the holes in his vest (the day was warm, and no one had his coat on but myself), pantaloons, drawers, and shirt, it appears evident that a ball must have been thrown from without, through the window, which entered his back on the right side, and passing through, lodged against his watch, which was in his right vest pocket, completely pulverizing the crystal and face, tearing off the hands and mashing the whole body of the watch. At the same instant the ball from the door entered his nose.

As he struck the floor he exclaimed emphatically, "I am a dead man." Joseph looked towards him and responded, "Oh, dear brother Hyrum!" and opening the door two or three inches with his left hand, discharged one barrel of a six shooter (pistol) at random in the entry, from whence a ball grazed Hyrum's breast, and entering his throat passed into his head, while other muskets were aimed at him and some balls hit him.

Joseph continued snapping his revolver round the casing of the door into the space as before, three barrels of which missed fire, while Mr. Taylor with a walking stick stood by his side and knocked down the bayonets and muskets which were constantly discharging through the doorway, while I stood by him, ready to lend any assistance, with another stick, but could not come within striking distance without going directly before the muzzle of the guns.

When the revolver failed, we had no more firearms, and

expected an immediate rush of the mob, and the doorway full of muskets, half way in the room, and no hope but instant death from within.

Mr. Taylor rushed into the window, which is some fifteen or twenty feet from the ground. When his body was nearly on a balance, a ball from the door within entered his leg, and a ball from without struck his watch, a patent lever, in his vest pocket near the left breast, and smashed it into "pie," leaving the hands standing at 5 o'clock, 16 minutes, and 26 seconds, the force of which ball threw him back on the floor, and he rolled under the bed which stood by his side, where he lay motionless, the mob from the door continuing to fire upon him, cutting away a piece of flesh from his left hip as large as a man's hand, and were hindered only by my knocking down their muzzles with a stick; while they continued to reach their guns into the room, probably left handed, and aimed their discharge so far round as almost to reach us in the corner of the room to where we retreated and dodged, and then I recommenced the attack with my stick.

Joseph attempted, as the last resort, to leap the same window from whence Mr. Taylor fell, when two balls pierced him from the door, and one entered his right breast from without, and he fell outward, exclaiming, "Oh Lord, my God!" As his feet went out of the window my head went in, the balls whistling all around. He fell on his left side a dead man.

At this instant the cry was raised, "He's leaped the window!" and the mob on the stairs and in the entry ran out.

I withdrew from the window, thinking it of no use to leap out on a hundred bayonets, then around General Joseph Smith's body.

Not satisfied with this I again reached my head out of the window, and watched some seconds to see if there were any signs of life, regardless of my own, determined to see the end of him I loved. Being fully satisfied that he was dead, with a hundred men near the body and more coming round the corner of the jail, and expecting a return to our room, I rushed towards the prison door, at the head of the stairs, and through the entry from whence the firing had proceeded, to learn if the doors into the prison were open.

When near the entry, Mr. Taylor called out, "Take me." I

pressed my way until I found all doors unbarred, returning instantly, caught Mr. Taylor under my arm and rushed by the stairs into the dungeon, or inner prison, stretched him on the floor and covered him with a bed in such a manner as not likely to be perceived, expecting an immediate return of the mob.

I said to Mr. Taylor, "This is a hard case to lay you on the floor, but if your wounds are not fatal, I want you to live to tell the story." I expected to be shot the next moment, and stood before the door awaiting the onset.[1]

While Willard Richards and John Taylor were in the cell, a company of the mob again rushed up stairs, but finding only the dead body of Hyrum, they were again descending the stairs, when a loud cry was heard, "The Mormons are coming!" which caused the whole band of murderers to flee . . . to the woods.[2]

Dr. Richards' escape was miraculous; he being a very large man, and in the midst of a shower of balls, yet he stood unscathed, with the exception of a ball which grazed the tip end of the lower part of his left ear. His escape fulfilled literally a prophecy which Joseph made over a year previously, that the time would come that the balls would fly around him like hail, and he should see his friends fall on the right and on the left, but that there should not be a hole in his garment.[3]

Death is sweet to the righteous

The Lord revealed to Joseph that not everyone who receives a priesthood blessing will be healed. The instructions are clear and beautiful, and bring joy and peace to those who have had to suffer the death of a loved one.

And whosoever among you are sick, and have not faith to be healed, but believe, shall be nourished with all tenderness, with herbs and mild food. . . .

And the elders of the church, two or more, shall be called, and shall pray for and lay their hands upon them in my name; and if they die they shall die unto me, and if they live they shall live unto me.

Thou shalt live together in love, insomuch that thou shalt weep for the loss of them that die, and more especially for those that have not hope of a glorious resurrection.

And it shall come to pass that those that die in me shall not taste of death, for it shall be sweet unto them;

And they that die not in me, wo unto them, for their death is bitter.

And again, it shall come to pass that he that hath faith in me to be healed, and is not appointed unto death, shall be healed. (D&C 42:43–48.)

"If you kill us, we shall be happy"

Joseph's mother, Lucy Mack Smith, had the following experience:

I beheld a large company of armed men advancing towards the city. . . .

Presently the main body came to a halt. The officers dismounting, eight of them came into the house. . . . I offered them chairs, but they refused to be seated. . . . They replied, "We do not choose to sit down; we have come here to kill Joe Smith and all the 'Mormons'. . . . We were sent to kill the Prophet and all who believe in him, and I'll be d—d if I don't execute my orders."

"I suppose," said I, "you intend to kill me, with the rest?"

"Yes, we do," returned the officer.

"Very well," I continued, "I want you to act the gentleman about it, and do the job quick. Just shoot me down at once, then I shall be at rest; but I should not like to be murdered by inches."

"There it is again," said he. "You tell a 'Mormon' that you will kill him, and they will always tell you, 'that is nothing—if you kill us, we shall be happy.' "[4]

Years later, as Joseph's followers pursued their weary way along the trail on their westward exodus from Nauvoo to the Salt Lake Valley, William Clayton expressed this optimism in the words of his beautiful hymn: "Come, come, ye Saints, no toil nor labor fear; but with joy wend your way. . . . And should we die before our journey's through, happy day, all is well!"[5]

"I am as liable to die as other men"

To many, Joseph appeared to be invincible. Indeed he had said: "I defy all the world to destroy the work of God; and I prophesy they never will have power to kill me till my work is accomplished, and I am ready to die."[6] But Joseph knew his fate. He knew he was to face a martyr's death.

Brigham Young said, "I heard Joseph say many a time, 'I shall not live until I am forty years of age."[7] Mary Elizabeth Rollins Lightner reported Joseph as saying, "I must seal my testimony to this generation with my blood."[8]

Although a prophet's work is probably never finished, Joseph knew he had sealed upon the heads of the Quorum of the Twelve "every key, every power, and every principle which the Lord has sealed upon my head"; and he could with confidence say to them, "I tell you, the burden of this kingdom now rests upon your shoulders; you have got to bear it . . . in all the world."[9] He said: "Some have supposed that Brother Joseph could not die, but this is a mistake: it is true there have been times when I have had the promise of my life to accomplish such and such things, but, having now accomplished those things, I have not at present any lease of my life, I am as liable to die as other men."[10]

Counsel for those who have lost a loved one

Joseph was no stranger to death. He and Emma had nine children, of whom five died either at birth or in infancy. They also lost an adopted son to death in his childhood. Joseph lost a brother when he was four and another when he was eighteen. Although he was killed in his thirty-ninth year, he had lived long enough to see his father die for the cause of truth; and for that cause one brother died with Joseph and another a few weeks later.

Messages of comfort cheered him in his time of sorrow. The Lord speaking to Joseph, and all who have cause to mourn, said:

> And now, verily I say unto you, and what I say unto one I say unto all, be of good cheer, little children; for I am in your midst, and I have not forsaken you;

And inasmuch as you have humbled yourselves before me, the blessings of the kingdom are yours.

Gird up your loins and be watchful and be sober, looking forth for the coming of the Son of Man, for he cometh in an hour you think not.

Pray always that you enter not into temptation, that you may abide the day of his coming, whether in life or in death. Even so. Amen. (D&C 61:36–39.)

The King Follett funeral message: a revelation of eternal truth about immortality

On Sunday, April 7, 1844, Joseph gave one of the greatest messages ever given, at the funeral of his friend King Follett, who had been accidentally crushed while digging a well. Of the Prophet's great sermon, George Q. Cannon said:

He [Joseph] chose for his subject the death of Elder King Follett, who had died a few days before, and he uplifted the souls of the congregation to a higher comprehension of the glory which comes after death to the faithful. His address ceased to be a mere eulogy of an individual, and became a revelation of eternal truths concerning the glories of immortality. The address occupied three hours and a half in delivery, and the multitude were held spellbound by its power. The Prophet seemed to rise above the world. It was as if the light of heaven already encircled his physical being. . . . Those who heard that sermon never forgot its power. Those who read it today think of it as an exhibition of superhuman power and eloquence.[11]

Following are a few salient points selected from the great truths the Prophet explained on that occasion.[12]

1. The Character of God

God himself was once as we are now, and is an exalted man, and sits enthroned in yonder heavens! That is the great secret. If the veil were rent today, and the great God who holds this world in its orbit, and who upholds all worlds and all things by his power, were to make himself visible,—I say, if you were to see him today, you would see him like a man in form—like yourselves in all the person, image, and very form as a man; for Adam was created in the very fashion, image and likeness of God, and received instruction from, and walked, talked and conversed with him as one man talks and communes with another. . . .

It is the first principle of the gospel to know for a certainty the Character of God, and to know that we may converse with Him as one man converses with another, and that He was once a man like us; yea, that God himself the Father of us all, dwelt on an earth, the same as Jesus Christ Himself did.

2. Men and Women Can Become Gods

Here, then is eternal life—to know the only wise and true God; and you have got to learn how to be gods yourselves, and to be kings and priests to God, the same as all gods have done before you, namely, by going from one small degree to another, and from a small capacity to a great one; from grace to grace, from exaltation to exaltation, until you . . . are able to dwell in everlasting burnings, and to sit in glory, as do those who sit enthroned in everlasting power.

3. Eternal Progress Requires Eternal Work—Faith Without Works Is Dead

When you climb up a ladder, you must begin at the bottom, and ascend step by step, until you arrive at the top; so it is with the principles of the gospel—you must begin with the first, and go on until you learn all the principles of exaltation. But it will be a great while after you have passed through the veil before you will have learned them. It is not all to be comprehended in this world; it will be a great work to learn our salvation and exaltation even beyond the grave.

4. We Can Help the Departed Attain Eternal Life

The greatest responsibility in this world that God has laid upon us is to seek after our dead. The apostle [Paul] says, "They without us cannot be made perfect"; for it is necessary that the sealing power should be in our hands to seal our children and our dead for the fulness of the dispensation of times—a dispensation to meet the promises made by Jesus Christ before the foundation of the world for the salvation of man.

5. Salvation Comes by Knowledge and Obedience

Knowledge saves a man; and in the world of spirits no man can be exalted but by knowledge. So long as a man will not give heed to the commandments, he must abide without salvation. If a man has knowledge, he can be saved; although, if he has been guilty of great sins, he will be punished for them. But when he consents to obey the gospel, whether here or in the world of spirits, he is saved.

6. Friends and Family Shall Be Together in the Celestial World

I am authorized to say, by the authority of the Holy Ghost, that you have no occasion to fear; for [King Follett] is gone to the home of the just. Don't mourn, don't weep. I know it by the testimony of the Holy Ghost that is within me; and you may wait for your friends to come forth to meet you in the morn of the celestial world.

Joseph added:

This is good doctrine. It tastes good. I can taste the principles of eternal life, and so can you. They are given to me by the revelations of Jesus Christ; and I know that when I tell you these words of eternal life as they are given to me, you taste them, and I know that you believe them. You say honey is sweet, and so do I. I can also taste the spirit of eternal life. I know that it is good; and when I tell you of these things which were given me by inspiration of the Holy Spirit, you are bound to receive them as sweet, and rejoice more and more.

Elder B. H. Roberts wrote: "The Prophet lived his life in *crescendo.* From small beginnings, it rose in breadth and power as he neared its close. As a teacher he reached the climax of his career in this discourse [the King Follett funeral sermon]. After it there was but one thing more he could do—seal his testimony with his blood. This he did less than three months later. Such is not the manner of life of false prophets."[13]

During the Millennium mothers will rear their resurrected children

Sister M. Isabella Horne said:

In conversation with the Prophet Joseph Smith once in Nauvoo, the subject of children in the resurrection was broached. I believe it was in Sister Leonora Cannon Taylor's house. She had just lost one of her children, and I had also lost one previously. The Prophet wanted to comfort us, and he told us that we should receive those children in the morning of the resurrection just as we laid them down, in purity and innocence, and we should nourish and care for them as their mothers. He said that children would be raised in the resurrection just as they were laid down, and that they would obtain all the intelligence necessary to occupy thrones, principalities and powers. The idea that I got from what he said was that the children would grow and develop in the Millennium, and that the mothers would have the pleasure of training and caring for them, which they had been deprived of in this life.

This was sometime after the King Follett funeral, at which I was present.

Brother Joseph Horne said:

I heard the Prophet Joseph Smith say that mothers should receive their children just as they laid them down, and that they would have the privilege of doing for them what they could not do here. The Prophet remarked: "How would you know them if you did not receive them as you laid them down?" I also got the idea that children would grow and develop after the resurrection, and that the mothers would care for them and train them.

In the *Improvement Era* for June, 1904, President Joseph F. Smith in an editorial on the resurrection said:

"The body will come forth as it is laid to rest, for there is no growth or development in the grave. As it is laid down, so will it arise, and changes to perfection will come by the law of restitution. But the spirit will continue to expand and develop, and the body, after the resurrection, will develop to the full stature of man."[14]

Death is but a small matter if we are prepared for the change

Joseph taught that "the only difference between the old and young dying is, one lives longer in heaven and eternal light and glory than the other, and is freed a little sooner from this miserable, wicked world."[15]

Brigham Young, in talking to the Saints about the death of their beloved Prophet, added:

It is but a small matter for us to lay down our lives if we are prepared for the change . . . if humility and faithfulness has characterized our lives, our condition will be much better than the present.[16]

We shall turn round and look upon it [the valley of death] and think, when we have crossed it, why this is the greatest advantage of my whole existence, for I have passed from a state of sorrow . . . and disappointment into a state of existence, where I can enjoy life to the fullest extent as far as that can be done without a body.

My spirit is set free. I thirst no more, I want to sleep no more, I hunger no more, I tire no more, I run, I walk, I labor . . . I am full of life, full of vigor, and I enjoy the presence of my heavenly Father, by the power of his Spirit.[17]

What is Joseph doing in the spirit world?

President Wilford Woodruff, the fourth President of the Church, saw Joseph in a night vision about the spirit world. In a talk given October 19, 1896, President Woodruff said:

In the night vision I saw him [Joseph Smith] at the door of the temple in heaven. He came to me and spoke to me. He said he could not stop to talk with me because he was in a hurry. . . .

I met half a dozen brethren who had held high positions on earth, and none of them could stop to talk with me because they were in a hurry. I was much astonished. By and by I saw the Prophet again and I got the privilege of asking him a question.

"Now," said I, "I want to know why you are in a hurry. I have been in a hurry all my life; but I expected my hurry would be over when I got into the kingdom of heaven, if I ever did."

Joseph said: "I will tell you, Brother Woodruff. Every dispensation that has had the priesthood on the earth and has gone into the celestial kingdom has had a certain amount of work to do to prepare to go to the earth with the Savior when he goes to reign on the earth.

"Each dispensation has had ample time to do this work. We have not. We are the last dispensation, and so much work has to be done, and we need to be in a hurry in order to accomplish it."[18]

5

Faith

Miracles are the fruits of faith![1]

—Joseph Smith

Faith comes by hearing the word of God, through the testimony of the servants of God.[2]

—Joseph Smith

Water for Zion's Camp

Brother Zera Cole was with Zion's Camp, which went up to Missouri in 1834. O. B. Huntington related the following story as detailed to him by Zera Cole:

> While traveling across a vast prairie, treeless and waterless, they encamped at night after a long and wearisome day's march. They had been without water since early morning, and men and animals suffered greatly from thirst, for it had been one of the hottest days of June.
>
> Joseph sat in his tent door looking out upon the scene. All at once he called for a spade. When it was brought he looked about him and selected a spot, the most convenient in the camp for men and teams to get water. Then he dug a shallow well, and immediately the water came bubbling up into it and filled it, so that the horses and mules could stand upon the brink and drink from it.
>
> While the camp stayed there, the well remained full, despite the fact that about two hundred men and scores of horses and mules were supplied from it.[3]

"Faith is the moving cause of all action"

Joseph taught: "[Paul] the author of the epistle to the Hebrews, in the eleventh chapter and first verse, gives the following definition of the word faith: 'Now faith is the substance (assurance) of things hoped for, the evidence of things not seen.'

"From this we learn that faith is the assurance which men have of the existence of things which they have not seen, and the principle of action in all intelligent beings. . . . It is faith, and faith only, which is the moving cause of all action . . . without it both mind and body would be in a state of inactivity . . . both physical and mental. . . . As faith is the moving cause of all action in temporal concerns, so it is in spiritual."[4]

"Trifle not with sacred things"

Through Joseph, the Lord taught Oliver Cowdery that he should "trifle not with sacred things" (D&C 6:12). Also, in 1829, before the Church was organized, he repeated his instruction to Oliver: "Remember that without faith, you can do nothing; therefore, ask in faith. Trifle not with these things; do not ask for that which you ought not." (D&C 8:10.)

At a later date Joseph said: "The Lord once told me that what I asked for I should have. I have been afraid to ask God to kill my enemies, lest some of them should, peradventure, repent." He also said: "I asked a short time since for the Lord to deliver me out of the hands of the governor; and if it needs must be to accomplish it to take him away; and the next news that came pouring down . . . was that Governor Reynolds had shot himself."[5]

"The Lord will let me live, if I am faithful to the promise which I made to him"

Joseph knew from translating the writings of Ether in the Book of Mormon that faith precedes the miracle: "For if there be no faith among the children of men God can do no miracle among them. . . . And neither at any time hath any wrought miracles until after their faith; wherefore they first believed in the Son of God." (Ether 12:12, 18.)

But perhaps Joseph learned something of the real power of faith from an experience that happened to his mother, Lucy Mack Smith. Many times he must have listened to the story of how his mother had been miraculously healed when she had committed to the Lord that she would be a support and comfort to "her husband and children" if he would let her live.

It was about three years before Joseph was born, and the family lived in Randolph, Vermont, where Joseph Smith, Sr., had opened a small store. They had two sons, Alvin, four, and Hyrum, two. Lucy caught a heavy cold which developed into a severe fever and her state deteriorated until "the physician pronounced [her] case to be confirmed consumption." She tells her story:

> I continued to grow weaker and weaker until I could scarcely endure even a foot-fall upon the floor. . . .
>
> While I was in this situation . . . I fancied to myself that [a visiting local minister] was going to ask me if I was prepared to die, and I dreaded to have him speak to me for then I did not consider myself ready for such an awful event, inasmuch as I knew not the ways of Christ. . . .
>
> When I was meditating upon death in this manner . . . my husband came to my bed and took me by the hand and said, "Oh, Lucy! my wife! my wife! you must die! The doctors have given you up, and all say you cannot live."
>
> I then looked to the Lord and begged and pleaded with him to spare my life in order that I might bring up my children and be a comfort to my husband. . . .
>
> During this night I made a solemn covenant with God that if He would let me live I would endeavor to serve him according to the best of my abilities. Shortly after this I heard a voice say to me, "Seek, and ye shall find; knock, and it shall be opened unto you. Let your heart be comforted; ye believe in God, believe also in me."
>
> In a few moments my mother came in and, looking upon me, she said, "Lucy, you are better."
>
> I replied, as my speech returned just at that instant, "Yes, mother, the Lord will let me live, if I am faithful to the promise which I made to him, to be a comfort to my mother, my husband, and my children." I continued to gain strength until I became quite well as to my bodily health, but my mind was considerably disquieted. It was wholly

occupied upon the subject of religion. As soon as I was able I made all diligence in endeavoring to find someone who was capable of instructing me more perfectly in the way of life and salvation.

Lucy knew she had promised God that she would find his Son, Jesus Christ. So as much as her health and care for her little family would permit, she went from church to church, from minister to minister, and searched the Bible with great diligence. But the more she heard ministers discourse, the more she became convinced in her heart "that there was not then upon earth the religion which I sought."

Though she was convinced in her heart that the true church was not upon the earth, she continued to study the Bible as her "guide to life and salvation." From her study of the Bible, she knew the importance of baptism. "At length I considered it my duty to be baptized . . . I stepped forward and yielded obedience to this ordinance, after which I continued to read the Bible."[6]

Little did Lucy realize what the Lord would require of her during her lifetime. She would lose two babies to death. She would see a son in his twenties die of illness, a son and her husband pass away from illness contracted due to fatigue and exposure from persecution, and two sons killed as martyrs by bullets from face-painted mobs. Joseph Smith, Sr., once said to his wonderful Lucy: "Mother, do you not know, that you are one of the most singular women in the world?"[7]

Lucy lived to the age of eighty and passed away in May of 1856, firm to the end in her testimony that her son Joseph was God's Prophet of the last dispensation.

The Zion's Camp march was a trial of their faith

The Lord chose the two hundred men who volunteered for Zion's Camp not to form a great army to right the wrongs suffered by the Saints in Missouri, but to teach and prepare "my warriors, my young men, and middle-aged" (D&C 105:16) for the trials that lay ahead of them: "That they themselves may be prepared, and that my people may be taught more perfectly, and have experience, and know more perfectly concerning their duty, and the things which I require at their hands" (D&C 105:10).

Then the Lord promised them that they would not have to fight to redeem Zion, but that he had sent the destroyer "to destroy and lay waste mine enemies"; and that he did not "require at their hands to fight the battles of Zion; for . . . I will fight your battles." (D&C 105:14–15.)

The following accounts show examples of how the Lord fulfilled his promise:

When the mob leaders of Jackson County heard that Zion's Camp was an armed force coming to Missouri to support the Saints, they started for Independence with Owens and Campbell in the lead, swearing they would raise an armed force of sufficient strength to annihilate the Mormon army en route to Clay County. Campbell swore, as he adjusted his pistols, "The eagles and turkey buzzards shall eat my flesh if I do not fix Joe Smith and his army so that their skins will not hold shucks, before two days are passed."[8]

He and eleven of his companions went to the ferry and started across the river about dusk, and "the angel of God saw fit to sink the boat about the middle of the river, and seven out of twelve that had attempted to cross, were drowned." The body of Campbell floated downstream "some four or five miles, and lodged upon a pile of drift wood, where the eagles, buzzards, ravens, crows, and wild animals ate his flesh from his bones, to fulfill his own words, and left him a horrible example of God's vengeance."[9] About three weeks later his bleaching bones were found by a Mr. Purtle.

Within about eighty miles of their destination, the camp was met by Bishop Edward Partridge, who reported on the Missourians' hostile feelings and prejudice against the Mormons. That night Lyman Wight baptized Dean Gould, the only non-Mormon of Zion's Camp.[10] While the brethren were making preparations for the night, five heavily armed men rode into the encampment and swore that the Mormons would "see hell before morning." "Such horrible oaths came from their lips," said one member of the camp, "I never heard before."[11]

The five Missourians boasted that sixty men were riding out from Richmond and seventy more from Clay County to join about two hundred Jackson County mobbers, and that all had avowed to utterly destroy "Joe Smith and his army."[12] Heber C. Kimball wrote, "The whole country was in a rage against us, and nothing but the power of God could save us."[13]

Soon after the five men left the camp, swearing vengeance,

a storm arose with tremendous fury; wind, rain, and hail struck the Jackson mob, softening their courage and frustrating their plans "to kill Joe Smith and his army." Very little hail fell in the camp of Zion's army, but for a mile around the hailstones cut down crops of corn and vegetation, even tearing limbs from trees. That night the river rose forty feet.

The Prophet Joseph, in telling of the incident, said:

> It seemed as if the mandate of vengeance had gone forth from the God of battles, to protect His servants from the destruction of their enemies, for the hail fell on them and not on us, and we suffered no harm, except the blowing down of some of our tents and getting wet; while our enemies had holes made in their hats, and otherwise received damage, even the breaking of their rifle stocks, and the fleeing of their horses through fear and pain.[14]

The next morning, Joseph was able to speak to some of the leaders of Ray County. He told them that the true objective of Zion's Camp was solely to help their stricken brethren in Missouri. The camp had only brought firearms for self-defense. The Mormons were not there to fight, but were looking for a settlement, and that they wanted to live in peace and desired to be permanent citizens of Missouri.

Parley P. Pratt declared that if Joseph Smith could once get the listening ear of even his most bitter enemies, his innate eloquence, inspired by the spirit of truth and the pathos of the Saints' sufferings, usually overwhelmed them.[15] In no instance was his triumph more pronounced than that morning at Little Fishing River.

"What have you accomplished?" was the sneering taunt of those weak in faith to members of Zion's Camp upon their return to Kirtland. "Just all we went for," came the reply of men such as Brigham Young, Heber C. Kimball, and George A. Smith. Brigham added, "I would not exchange the experience I gained in that expedition for all the wealth in Geauga County"—the county in which Kirtland was then located.[16]

Wilford Woodruff, a priest when he walked to Missouri with Zion's Camp, later declared:

> We gained an experience that we never could have gained in any other way. We had the privilege of beholding the face of

the prophet, and we had the privilege of travelling one thousand miles with him and seeing the workings of the Spirit of God with him, and the revelations of Jesus Christ unto him and the fulfillment of those revelations. . . . Had I not gone up with Zion's Camp, I should not have been here today.[17]

"Without faith you can do nothing"

Through Joseph Smith, the Lord told Oliver Cowdery, "without faith you can do nothing" (D&C 8:10). Or, as the angel Gabriel said to Mary, "Fear not. . . . For with God nothing shall be impossible" (Luke 1:30, 37).

Many of the early missionaries of the Church met with tremendous success in foreign lands, even though they didn't know how to speak the language of the people. One such story is told of Elders Franklin D. Richards and Karl G. Maeser, two men prominent in the history of the Church.

When they first met, they conversed, one speaking English and the other German, and although neither understood the language of the other, except imperfectly, both were in such accord with each other that Elder Maeser grasped the instructions Elder Richards imparted to him, and he rejoiced greatly, as one truth after another was unfolded to him in this manner. "Without faith you can do nothing," but by faith frail man may draw, as it were, on the unlimited resources and power of the Almighty.[18]

The Lord told his young elders how to preach the gospel:

Verily I say unto you, he that is ordained of me and sent forth to preach the word of truth by the Comforter, in the Spirit of truth, doth he preach it by the Spirit of truth or some other way?

And if it be by some other way it is not of God.

And again, he that receiveth the word of truth, doth he receive it by the Spirit of truth or some other way?

If it be some other way it is not of God.

Therefore, why is it that ye cannot understand and know, that he that receiveth the word by the Spirit of truth receiveth it as it is preached by the Spirit of truth?

Wherefore, he that preacheth and he that receiveth, understand one another, and both are edified and rejoice together. (D&C 50:17–22.)

"I wonder if we are doing all we can"

In reviewing the success of the early missionaries, President Spencer W. Kimball said:

When I read Church history, I am amazed at the boldness of the early brethren as they went out into the world. They seemed to find a way. Even in persecution and hardship, they opened doors which evidently have been allowed to sag on their hinges and many of them to close.

I remember that these fearless men were teaching the gospel in Indian lands before the Church was even fully organized. As early as 1837, the Twelve were in England fighting Satan, in Tahiti in 1844, Australia in 1851, Iceland 1853, Italy 1850, and also in Switzerland, Germany, Tonga, Turkey, Mexico, Japan, Czechoslovakia, China, Samoa, New Zealand, South America, France, and Hawaii in 1850. . . .

Much of this early proselyting was done while the leaders were climbing the Rockies and planting the sod and starting their homes. It is faith and super faith.

President Kimball asked,

I wonder if we are doing all we can? Are we complacent in our approach to teaching all the world? . . . Are we prepared to lengthen our stride? To enlarge our vision? . . . Somehow, brethren, I feel that when we have done all in our power that the Lord will find a way to open doors. That is my faith![19]

"Did I not tell you the Lord would send me some money to help us on our journey?"

When Joseph and the other Saints in Kirtland heard of the suffering of their friends in Missouri, they wanted to help. The Lord commanded Joseph that at least one hundred of "the strength of my house" (D&C 103:22, 30) be gathered to go as an army of the Lord to help. Many more than one hundred gathered, but there was little money available to help them make the journey. Wilford Woodruff, a convert of only four months, recorded in his journal:

> He [Joseph] said, . . . "Brethren, don't be discouraged about our not having means. The Lord will provide, and He will put it into the heart of somebody to send me some money." The very next day he received a letter from Sister Vose, containing one hundred and fifty dollars. When he opened the letter and took out the money, he held it up and exclaimed: "See here, did I not tell you the Lord would send me some money to help us on our journey? Here it is." I felt satisfied that Joseph was a Prophet of God in very deed.[20]

Faith to be healed

> A young lady, by the name of Chloe Smith, being a member of the Church, was lying very low with a lingering fever. . . . Many of the Church had visited and prayed with her, but all to no effect; she seemed at the point of death, but would not consent to have a physician. This greatly enraged her relatives, who had cast her out because she belonged to the Church, and who, together with many of the people of the neighborhood, were greatly stirred up to anger, saying, "these wicked deceivers will let her lie and die without a physician, because of their superstitions; and if they do, we will prosecute them for so doing." Now these were daily watching for her last breath, with many threats.
>
> Under these circumstances, President Smith and myself [Parley P. Pratt], with several other Elders, called to see her. . . .
>
> We kneeled down and prayed vocally all around, each in turn; after which President Smith arose, went to the bedside, took her by the hand, and said unto her with a loud voice: "in the name of Jesus Christ arise and walk!"
>
> She immediately arose, was dressed by a woman in attendance, when she walked to a chair before the fire, and was seated and joined in singing a hymn. The house was thronged with people in a few moments, and the young lady arose and shook hands with each as they came in; and from that minute she was perfectly restored to health.[21]

"Moroni, Joseph's Tutor," by Clark Kelley Price.
Courtesy of Delbert and Rama Cheney of Star Valley, Wyoming.

6

Family Life

Pray in your families unto the Father, always in my name, that your wives and your children may be blessed.
—3 Nephi 18:21

And ye will not suffer your children that they go hungry, or naked; neither will ye suffer that they transgress the laws of God, and fight and quarrel one with another, and serve the devil. . . .

But ye will teach them to walk in the ways of truth and soberness; ye will teach them to love one another, and to serve one another.
—Mosiah 4:14–15

"Could not have conceived the idea in his mind"

It is interesting to note that the first persons who believed in the miraculous events related by the young man Joseph Smith were the members of his own family, his father and mother and brothers and sisters. Not one of them doubted him. In an article written for publication in 1875, Joseph's brother William made the following statement:

"Joseph Smith, at the age of 17 years, with the moral training he had received from strictly pious and religious parents, could not have conceived the idea in his mind of palming off a fabulous story, such as seeing angels, etc. . . .

"There was not a single member of the family of sufficient age to know right from wrong but what had implicit confidence in the statements made by my brother Joseph, concerning his vision and the knowledge he thereby obtained concerning the plates."

Years later, in 1893, when William had become an old man, he was interviewed by members of the Reorganized Church. A certain "Brother Briggs" asked him the following question, "Did you not doubt Joseph's testimony sometimes?" To this question William replied:

"No, we all had the most implicit confidence in what he said. He was a truthful boy. Father and mother believed him; why should not the children? I suppose if he had told crooked stories about other things, we might have doubted his word about the plates, but Joseph was a truthful boy. That father and mother believed his report and suffered persecution for that belief shows that he was truthful. No, sir, we never doubted his word for a minute." (Journal History, Jan. 20, 1894.)

Throughout long years, filled with trouble, sorrow, disappointments and difficulties of the severest kind, not one member of Joseph Smith's family ever renounced belief in his divine calling. What strength and courage that gave him, during his brief lifetime, can hardly be estimated.[1]

My father told me it was of God and to go and do as commanded by the messenger

In Joseph Smith's history we read:

I shortly after arose from my bed, and, as usual, went to the necessary labors of the day; but, in attempting to work as at other times, I found my strength so exhausted as to render me entirely unable. My father, who was laboring along with me, discovered something to be wrong with me, and told me to go home. I started with the intention of going to the house; but, in attempting to cross the fence out of the field where we were, my strength entirely failed me, and I fell helpless on the ground, and for a time was quite unconscious of anything.

The first thing that I can recollect was a voice speaking unto me, calling me by name. I looked up, and beheld the same messenger standing over my head, surrounded by light as before. He then again related unto me all that he had related to me the previous night, and commanded me to go to my father and tell him of the vision and commandments which I had received.

I obeyed; I returned to my father in the field, and rehearsed the whole matter to him. He replied to me that it was of God, and told me to go and do as commanded by the mesenger. (Joseph Smith—History 1:48–50.)

Seated in a circle, father, mother, sons, and daughters giving attention to a boy prophet

Joseph's father was excited to learn what had happened to his son when he went to the Hill Cumorah and met the angel Moroni there for the first time. The events immediately following the visit of Moroni are well described by the Prophet's mother:

> The ensuing evening, when the family were altogether, Joseph made known to them all that he had communicated to his father in the field, and also of his finding the record, as well as what passed between him and the angel while he was at the place where the plates were deposited.
> . . . Alvin [suggested to Joseph] "If mother will get our suppers early [tomorrow], we will have a fine long evening, and we will all sit down for the purpose of listening to you while you tell us the great things which God has revealed to you."
> Accordingly, by sunset the next day, we were all seated, and Joseph commenced telling us the great and glorious things which God had manifested to him; but, before proceeding, he charged us not to mention out of the family that which he was about to say to us, as the world was so wicked that when they came to a knowledge of these things they would try to take our lives. . . .
> After giving us this charge, he proceeded to relate further particulars concerning the work which he was appointed to do, and we received them joyfully. . . .
> From this time forth, Joseph continued to receive instructions from the Lord, and we continued to get the children together every evening for the purpose of listening. . . .
> I presume our family presented an aspect as singular as any that ever lived upon the face of the earth—all seated in a circle, father, mother, sons and daughters, and giving the most profound attention to a boy, eighteen years of age, who had never read the Bible through in his life. . . .

We were now confirmed in the opinion that God was about to bring to light something upon which we could stay our minds, or that would give us a more perfect knowledge of the plan of salvation and the redemption of the human family. This caused us greatly to rejoice, the sweetest union and happiness pervaded our house, and tranquility reigned in our midst.[2]

"I am the mother of the Prophet"

A well-earned tribute to Lucy Mack Smith is recorded in the foreword to her book about her Prophet son:

Mrs. Smith experienced supreme pride and joy in the knowledge and realization that she was the mother of the Prophet of God. It was her pleasure to declare on numerous occasions, "I am the mother of the Prophet." No one except herself could have known the satisfaction she derived from this knowledge. And yet, she was called upon to pay the full price for this glorious privilege; poverty, persecution, trials, troubles and sorrows of the bitterest kind were to be her lot in this world. . . .

. . . Lucy Mack Smith's devotion to her gifted son, to the doctrines he taught, and to the organization he brought forth, was as pure as gold. The Church of Jesus Christ of Latter-day Saints never had a more devoted and loyal member than this good woman. Her place in history, as the "first woman of the Church," it seems to us, is secure.[3]

The last known discourse of Lucy Smith, Joseph's mother

Wednesday, October 8, 1845.—Conference opened at the usual hour with singing and prayer.

Mother Lucy Smith, the aged and honored parent of Joseph Smith, having expressed a wish to say a few words to the congregation, she was invited upon the stand. She spoke at considerable length and in an audible manner, so as to be heard by a large portion of the vast assembly.

She commenced by saying that she was truly glad that

the Lord had let her see so large a congregation. She had a great deal of advice to give. . . . There were comparatively few in the assembly who were acquainted with her family. She was the mother of eleven children, seven of whom were boys. She raised them in the fear and love of God, and never was there a more obedient family. She warned parents that they were accountable for their children's conduct; advised them to give them books and work to keep them from idleness; warned all to be full of love, goodness and kindness, and never to do in secret, what they would not do in the presence of millions.

She wished to know of the congregation whether they considered her a mother in Israel (upon which President Brigham Young said: all who consider Mother Smith as a mother in Israel, signify it by saying yes!—One universal "yes" rang throughout).

She remarked that it was just eighteen years since Joseph Smith the Prophet had become acquainted with the contents of the plates; and then in a concise manner related over the most prominent points in the early history of her family; their hardships, trials, privations, persecutions, sufferings, etc.; some parts of which melted those who heard her to tears, more especially the part relating to a scene in Missouri, when her beloved son Joseph was condemned to be shot in fifteen minutes, and she by prodigious efforts was enabled to press through the crowd to where he was, and to give him her hand; but could not see his face; he took her hand and kissed it; she said, let me hear your voice once more my son; he said, "God bless you my dear mother!"

She gave notice that she had written her history, [this later became known as *History of Joseph Smith by His Mother Lucy Mack Smith*] and wished it printed before we leave this place.

She then mentioned a discourse once delivered by Joseph after his return from Washington, in which he said that he had done all that could be done on earth to obtain justice for their wrongs; but they were all, from the president to the judge, determined not to grant justice. But, said he, keep good courage, these cases are recorded in heaven, and I am going to lay them before the highest court in heaven.

"Little," said she, "did I then think he was so soon to leave us, to take the case up himself. And don't you think this case is now being tried? I feel as though God was vexing this nation a little, here and there, and I feel that the Lord will let Brother Brigham take the people away.

"Here, in this city, lay my dead; my husband and children; and if so be the rest of my children go with you, (and would to God they may all go), they will not go without me; and if I go, I want my bones brought back in case I die away, and deposited with my husband and children."

(Mother Smith said many more good things, but the rest being inaudible to the reporters, they are lost.)

President Brigham Young then arose and said he wanted to relate to the congregation the last closing remarks of Mother Smith; inasmuch as she could not be heard by all.

"Mother Smith proposes a thing which rejoices my heart: she will go with us. I can answer for the authorities of the church; we want her and her children to go with us; and I pledge myself in behalf of the authorities of the church, that while we have anything, they shall share with us. We have extended the helping hand to Mother Smith. She has the best carriage in the city and while she lives, shall ride in it when and where she pleases. . . .

"Mother Smith has been relating over the circumstances of her pecuniary life of late; she is perfectly satisfied, and all is right. I could have wished that the bishops would visit her more frequently; but they have done pretty well—and I say in the name of the Latter-day Saints, we will supply her wants; and I want the people to take anything they have for her to her, and let her do with it as she pleases.

"I have never asked her to go for she had told me she would not; but now she has offered it. Mother Smith proposes that she will go with us, if we will promise to bring back her remains in case of her death and deposit them with her husband's. . . . And I pledge myself if Mother Smith goes with us and I outlive her, I will do my best to bring her bones back again, and deposit them with her children, and I want to know if this people are willing to enter into a covenant to do the same." (Unanimous vote.)[4]

When the Saints finally were forced to go west, Lucy decided against making the arduous journey. She stayed in

Nauvoo with Emma and Joseph's children. The mobs, who plagued them so much during her life, left her and Emma pretty much alone after the main body of the Saints left the city. She died near Nauvoo on May 14, 1856.

The value of a letter from home

Solomon, king of Israel, wrote in Proverbs: "As cold water to a thirsty soul, so is good news from a far country" (Proverbs 25:25).

Joseph spent the winter months, including the Christmas season of 1838, in Liberty Jail. After months of confinement, he received letters from home and his friends. He recorded his feelings:

> We received some letters last evening—one from Emma, one from Don C. Smith, and one from Bishop Partridge—all breathing a kind and consoling spirit. We were much gratified with their contents. We had been a long time without information; and when we read those letters they were to our souls as the gentle air is refreshing, but our joy was mingled with grief, because of the sufferings of the poor and much injured Saints.
>
> And we need not say to you that the floodgates of our hearts were lifted and our eyes were a fountain of tears, but those who have not been enclosed in the walls of prison without cause or provocation, can have but little idea how sweet the voice of a friend is.
>
> One token of friendship from any source whatever awakens and calls into action every sympathetic feeling; it brings up in an instant everything that is passed; it seizes the present with the avidity of lightning; it grasps after the future with the fierceness of a tiger; it moves the mind backward and forward, from one thing to another, until finally all enmity, malice and hatred, and past differences, misunderstandings and mismanagements are slain victorious at the feet of hope; and when the heart is sufficiently contrite, then the voice of inspiration steals along and whispers . . .[5]

"We always had family prayers"

Some who simply read Joseph Smith's history feel he must have come from a family where prayer was not a common practice. Their support for this belief comes from Joseph's statement: "It was the first time in my life that I had made such attempt [to pray], for amidst all my anxieties I had never as yet made the attempt to pray vocally. After I had retired to that place where I had previously designed to go, having looked around me, and finding myself alone, I kneeled down and began to offer up the desires of my heart to God." (Joseph Smith—History 1:14–15.)

The truth is that Joseph came from a religious family. They had daily scripture reading, family prayer, and a hymn. This is confirmed by the words of Joseph's younger brother William in a testimony given regarding the family. In an interview, William was asked: "Were your folks religiously inclined before Joseph saw the angel?" He replied:

Yes, we always had family prayers since I can remember. I well remember father used to carry his spectacles in his vest pocket, (feeling in his lower right hand pocket to show us how and where) and when us boys saw him feel for his specs, we knew that was a signal to get ready for prayer, and if we did not notice it, mother would say, "William," or whoever was the negligent one, "get ready for prayer." After the prayer we had a song we would sing, I remember part of it yet. "Another day has passed and gone, we lay our garments by."[6]

In the Book of Mormon the Lord Jesus Christ confirms the importance of family prayer. Individual prayer is essential, but so is family prayer, as it brings unity and strength. "Pray in your families unto the Father, always in my name [the name of Jesus Christ], that your wives and your children may be blessed" (3 Nephi 18:21).

Nephi gives a warning to us all: "If ye would hearken unto the Spirit which teacheth a man to pray ye would know that ye must pray; for the evil spirit teacheth not a man to pray, but teacheth him that he must not pray" (2 Nephi 32:8).

7

Friendship

Friendship is one of the grand fundamental principles of "Mormonism"; [it is designed] to revolutionize and civilize the world, and cause wars and contentions to cease and men to become friends and brothers.[1]

—Joseph Smith

I give unto you this commandment, that ye become even as my friends in days when I was with them, traveling to preach the gospel in my power.

—D&C 84:77

One of the wagon wheels came off

An experience of Joseph Smith's is recorded as follows:

We had appointed a meeting for this evening, for the purpose of attending to the confirmation of those who had been the same morning baptized. The time appointed had arrived and our friends had nearly all collected together, when to my surprise, I was visited by a constable, and arrested by him on a warrant, on the charge of being a disorderly person, of setting the country in an uproar by preaching the Book of Mormon, etc.

The constable informed me, soon after I had been arrested, that the plan of those who had got out the warrant was to get me into the hands of the mob, who were now lying in ambush for me, but that he was determined to save me from them, as he had found me to be a different sort of person from what I had been represented to him. I soon found that he had told me the truth in this matter, for not far from Mr. Knight's house, the wagon in which we had set out was surrounded by a mob, who seemed only to await some signal from the constable; but to their great disappointment, he gave the horse the whip, and drove me out of their reach.

Whilst driving in great haste one of the wagon wheels came off, which left us once more very nearly surrounded by them, as they had come on in close pursuit. However, we managed to replace the wheel and again left them behind us. He drove on to the town of South Bainbridge, Chenango county, where he lodged me for the time being in an upper room of a tavern; and in order that all might be right with himself and with me also, he slept during the night with his feet against the door, and a loaded musket by his side, whilst I occupied a bed which was in the room; he having declared that if we were interrupted unlawfully, he would fight for me, and defend me as far as it was in his power.[2]

"If my life is of no value to my friends it is of none to myself"

Some say that Joseph was too nice to others and often his friendship or generosity would get him into trouble. At times, even his best friends turned against him. He said that he understood how the Savior felt when his friends "laughed him to scorn" (Matthew 9:24).

Just a few days prior to his martyrdom in June of 1844, all of the powers of evil seemed to combine together to destroy the Saints or to create the environment where the blood of Joseph and Hyrum would be shed to stand as a testimony to the world of the truthfulness of the gospel. Joseph, Hyrum, and their friends, Porter Rockwell and Willard Richards, crossed the Mississippi at night in a leaky old rowboat, "baling out the water with their boots and shoes to prevent it from sinking." They were determined to go west to the Rocky Mountains and find a place of peace to establish Zion. Joseph told his friend Stephen Markham, "If I and Hyrum were ever taken again we should be massacred, or I am not a prophet of God."[3]

While safely on the Iowa side of the river, he received word from friends and a letter from his wife Emma. Some suggested cowardice had made him leave. They begged him to return and go to Carthage, where Governor Ford had promised his safety.

Joseph urged Hyrum not to go with him, but Hyrum would not be separated from his brother's side. "In life they were not divided, and in death they were not separated!" (D&C 135:3.) Therefore Joseph asked his friends to help them return to Nauvoo, saying: "If my life is of no value to my friends it is of none to myself."[4]

Thus at the insistence of friends he returned to Nauvoo and within a day or so made his way to Carthage, Illinois. Knowing well his fate, he said: "I am going like a lamb to the slaughter, but I am calm as a summer's morning. I have a conscience void of offense toward God and toward all men. If they take my life I shall die an innocent man . . . and it shall yet be said of me 'He was murdered in cold blood.' "[5]

Then on June 27, 1844, just past five o'clock in the late afternoon, a mob of between one hundred fifty and two hundred drunken men with painted faces stormed the Carthage Jail.[6] There Joseph and Hyrum sealed with their deaths their testimonies of the gospel of Jesus Christ as martyrs to his cause, thus confirming the Savior's profound statement: "Greater love hath no man than this, that a man lay down his life for his friends" (John 15:13).

"You may thank Joseph Smith for being alive"

At the time the Prophet Joseph Smith and some of his brethren were betrayed into the hands of the mob militia in Missouri, one of the mobocrats, General Moses Wilson,

> was hunting for testimony against the Prophet on the occasion of the trial by court-martial. He went to Lyman Wight. "Wight," he said, "we have nothing against you, only that you are associated with Joe Smith. He is our enemy and a damned rascal, and would take any plan he could to kill us. You are a damned fine fellow. If you will come out and swear against him, we will spare your life, and give you any office you want; and if you don't, you will be shot to-morrow at nine."
>
> "General Wilson," the redoubtable colonel answered, "you are entirely mistaken in your man, both in regard to myself and Joseph Smith. Joseph Smith is not an enemy to mankind. He is not your enemy. In fact, he is as good a

friend as you have. For had it not been for Joseph Smith, you would have been in hell long ago, and I would have sent you there myself by cutting your throat, and no other man but Joseph Smith could have prevented me. You may thank him for being alive. And now, if you will give me the boys I brought from Diahman [Adam-ondi-Ahman] yesterday, I will whip your whole army."

Wilson was silent for a moment. Then he said, "Wight, you're a strange man. But if you do not accept my proposal, you will be shot to-morrow morning at nine."

And Lyman answered, "Shoot, and be damned."[7]

"Judge, you will aspire to the presidency of the United States"

Joseph Smith was dining at Carthage, Illinois, with the thirty-year-old Judge Stephen A. Douglas and others. After dinner, Judge Douglas asked the Prophet to give him an account of the persecutions of the Saints in Missouri. Joseph did so, talking for almost three hours.

At the time the judge seemed to be very friendly towards the Prophet. When Joseph had told him all that the Saints had passed through, he looked straight into Mr. Douglas's face and said: "Judge, you will aspire to the presidency of the United States; and if you ever turn your hand against me or the Latter-day Saints, you will feel the weight of the hand of the Almighty upon you; and you will live to see and know that I have testified the truth to you; for the conversation of this day will stick to you through life."

Seventeen years afterwards, Mr. Douglas was nominated for the office of president of the United States. It was firmly believed that he would be elected, for he was looked upon as a great man, and in the preceding presidential election his party had polled over half a million votes more than the opposing parties. But in order to make friends of those who were opposed to the Saints, he turned against the Latter-day Saints and said many things about them that were false and wicked.

When the day of the election came Judge Douglas was soundly defeated; he was voted down in every state in the Union except one. Abraham Lincoln was elected president. In less than a year Stephen A. Douglas, only forty-eight years of age, died at his home in Chicago, a disappointed and broken-hearted man.[8]

"I feel like shouting hallelujah"

Brigham Young, whom Joseph learned to love and trust as a true friend, expressed his feelings for Joseph in a short but beautiful comment: "I feel like shouting hallelujah, all the time, when I think that I ever knew Joseph Smith."[9]

The Prophet Joseph Smith— a friend of children

Little Evaline Burdick sat on the floor of her family's small log cabin in Kirtland, Ohio. It was wash day, and there were clothes and bedding hanging outside on the line and drying on the lawn. She played happily while her mother tended to the washing.

Evaline saw a tall, handsome man with sandy hair walk up the steps of their front porch and enter the open door of their cabin. He greeted her mother and then picked Evaline up. He held her in his left arm and crossed the room to a large mirror. They both looked in the mirror and smiled at each other. Gently he set her back on the floor and asked where her father was.

When the kind man left the room, Evaline's mother called her over and told her that the man was Joseph Smith, a true prophet of the Lord. What a good man he was! Evaline would never forget that experience.

The Prophet Joseph Smith loved children. He was never too busy to stop and play with young people, to compliment them on something they had done, or to pick wildflowers for little girls. During the winter, he loved sliding on the ice with his own children and their friends.

When wagonloads of grown people and children came in from the countryside for church meetings, Joseph would make his way to the wagons and greet each person. He would pay special attention to the children, taking each of them tenderly by the hand and giving them his blessing.

Once, while Joseph was delivering a sermon in someone's

home, a little girl became tired and sleepy and began to cry. Joseph stopped speaking for a moment, sat down, and motioned for her to come to him. He held her on his lap, patted her, and she went to sleep while he completed his sermon.

In Nauvoo, Illinois, in 1843, the Prophet saw a young boy, Jesse N. Smith, walk by his home. He called the boy to his side and asked him what book he was reading in school. When Jesse replied, "The Book of Mormon," Joseph was very happy and took him into the house and gave him a copy of the Book of Mormon for his very own. The boy treasured that gift the rest of his life.

Joseph loved to play a version of baseball with the young boys. He could knock the ball so far that the other players would tell the boy going after it to take his dinner along. Joseph would laugh and go on with the game.

The Prophet Joseph also taught young people the joy of serving others. Once, in Nauvoo, he and some young men were playing ball. When they began to get tired, he stopped the game, called them together, and said, "Let's build a log cabin." So off they went, Joseph and the young men, to build a log cabin for a widow.

Joseph understood Jesus' words when He said, "Suffer the little children to come unto me, and forbid them not: for of such is the kingdom of God" (Mark 10:14). Like Jesus, Joseph loved children. And children loved him.[10]

"He is our friend, and . . . He will save our souls"

In the winter of 1838, Joseph and several others were confined for a period of several months in Liberty Jail. Some of the members turned away from the Prophet and the Church during this period. However, the majority of the Saints had such a strong conviction about their Prophet that they would have followed him to their deaths if necessary.

It was upon these stalwart members that he fixed his attention once he settled down in the cold, dimly lighted quarters of the Liberty jail. Rather than wasting time bemoaning his fate, he set about to use the weapons at hand [a quill pen, a bottle of ink, and a precious pad of writing paper]. A stream of letters commenced to flow from him to members of his family and the brethren. These letters were devoid of even a hint of pessimism or self-pity; on the contrary, they breathed a spirit of buoyant self-confidence. In a letter addressed to the Church at large in December 1838 he wrote:

"Dear Brethren, do not think that our hearts faint, as though some strange thing had happened unto us, for we have seen and have been assured of all these things beforehand, and have an assurance of a better hope than that of our persecutors. Therefore God hath made broad our shoulders for the burden. We glory in our tribulation, because we know that God is with us, that He is our friend, and that He will save our souls."[11]

And to Emma he wrote: "God is my Friend; in him I shall find comfort. I have given my life into his hands. I am prepared to go at his call. I desire to be with Christ. I count not my life dear to me, only to do his will."[12]

"The Restoration of the Melchizedek Priesthood," by Kenneth Riley.
Used by permission of The Church of Jesus Christ of Latter-day Saints.

8

Honesty

We believe in being honest, true, chaste, benevolent, virtuous, and in doing good to all men; indeed, we may say that we follow the admonition of Paul—We believe all things, we hope all things, we have endured many things, and hope to be able to endure all things. If there is anything virtuous, lovely, or of good report or praiseworthy, we seek after these things.

—Articles of Faith 1:13

"My honor was at stake"

Joseph Smith was a man of great integrity. In the spring of 1843, he asked Thomas Colburn to lend him one hundred dollars in order to pay the lawyer who had defended his friend the falsely accused Porter Rockwell. Said Joseph of the money, "This shall be returned within three days, if I am alive." Thomas Colburn's daughter reported:

> My aunt, father's sister, was quite wrathful [after Joseph left]. "Don't you know, Thomas," said she, "you will never see a cent of that money again. Here are your family without a home, and you throw your money away." . . .
>
> The day came when it was to be paid—a cold, wet, rainy day. "The day passed. Night came—9 o'clock, 10 o'clock, and we all retired for the night. Shortly after there was a knock at the door. Father arose and went to it, and there in the driving rain stood the Prophet Joseph [with the money in gold]. He said, "Brother Thomas, I have been trying all day to raise this sum, for my honor was at stake. God bless you."[1]

"He was a truthful boy"

In 1893, William Smith, Joseph's only living brother, was asked, "Did you not doubt Joseph's testimony sometimes?" To which he replied:

No, we all had the most implicit confidence in what he said. He was a truthful boy. Father and mother believed him; why should not the children? I suppose if he had told crooked stories about other things, we might have doubted his word about the plates, but Joseph was a truthful boy. That father and mother believed his report and suffered persecution for that belief shows that he was truthful. No, sir, we never doubted his word for a minute.[2]

"I know him to be an honest man"

At length the trial commenced amidst a multitude of spectators, who in general evinced a belief that I was guilty of all that had been reported concerning me, and of course were very zealous that I should be punished according to my crimes. Among many witnesses called . . . was Mr. Josiah Stoal—of whom I have made mention as having worked for him some time—and examined to the following effect:

"Did not the prisoner, Joseph Smith, have a horse of you?"

"Yes."

"Did not he go to you and tell you that an angel had appeared unto him and authorized him to get the horse from you?"

"No, he told me no such story."

"Well, how had he the horse of you?"

"He bought him of me as any other man would."

"Have you had your pay?"

"That is not your business."

The question being again put, the witness replied:

"I hold his note for the price of the horse, which I consider as good as the pay; for I am well acquainted with Joseph Smith, Jun., and know him to be an honest man; and if he wishes, I am ready to let him have another horse on the same terms."[3]

"You thirst for blood, and nothing but my blood will satisfy you"

Joseph Smith was so honest that he had to tell the truth even when perhaps it incited mobs and others to plan his death. One such instance occurred just two days before his death in Carthage:

> Several of the officers of the troops in Carthage, and other gentlemen, curious to see the Prophet, visited Joseph in his room. [Joseph] asked them if there was anything in his appearance that indicated he was the desperate character his enemies represented him to be; and he asked them to give him their honest opinion on the subject.
>
> The reply was, "No, sir, your appearance would indicate the very contrary, General Smith; but we cannot see what is in your heart, neither can we tell what are your intentions."
>
> To which Joseph replied, "Very true, gentlemen, you cannot see what is in my heart, and you are therefore unable to judge me or my intentions; but I can see what is in your hearts, and will tell you what I see. I can see that you thirst for blood, and nothing but my blood will satisfy you. It is not for crime of any description that I and my brethren are thus continually persecuted and harassed by our enemies, but there are other motives, and some of them I have expressed, so far as relates to myself.
>
> And inasmuch as you and the people thirst for blood, I prophesy, in the name of the Lord, that you shall witness scenes of blood and sorrow to your entire satisfaction. Your souls shall be perfectly satiated with blood, and many of you who are now present shall have an opportunity to face the cannon's mouth from sources you think not of; and those people that desire this great evil upon me and my brethren, shall be filled with regret and sorrow because of the scenes of desolation and distress that await them. They shall seek for peace, and shall not be able to find it. Gentlemen, you will find what I have told you to be true."[4]

Joseph's prophecy was to be fulfilled. Much has been said and written about the afflictions sustained by those who took part in the betrayal and martyrdom of Joseph Smith, the Prophet of God.[5]

He told his friends the truth

The Lord reiterated the principle of honesty when he said, "I, the Lord, promise the faithful and cannot lie" (D&C 62:6). Honesty includes speaking the truth to those we love.

The Lord also told Joseph, "My people must needs be chastened until they learn obedience, if it must needs be, by the things which they suffer" (D&C 105:6). However, he warned Joseph that although he must reprove "betimes with sharpness, when moved upon by the Holy Ghost," Joseph was to "[show] forth afterwards an increase of love toward him whom he hast reproved, lest he esteem thee to be his enemy" (D&C 121:43).

> [Doctrine and Covenants] revelations are remarkable because in them men are told of their sins and admonished to repent. This is one mark of their divine origin. If the Prophet Joseph Smith had been an impostor, it would have been immaterial to him whether his associates were humble or proud; whether they were looking for the approbation of the world, or not. He would not have rebuked them, as he did, at the risk of losing their support. He could not have admonished them to repent, for they would have known of his true character. But he was no impostor. He told his friends the truth, and they knew that the Spirit of God spoke through him. This is proof of his divine calling, for it is one of the functions of a Prophet of God to show His people their sins. Micah 3:8.[6]

The Lord, through Joseph, was also quick to compliment those who were honest: "Blessed is my servant Hyrum Smith; for I, the Lord, love him because of the integrity of his heart, and because he loveth that which is right before me, saith the Lord. . . . George Miller is without guile; he may be trusted because of the integrity of his heart; and for the love which he has to my testimony I, the Lord, love him." (D&C 124:15, 20.)

It should be the goal of all of us to have it said, "I, the Lord, love him because of the integrity of his heart and his love for me."

"It is my will that you shall pay all your debts"

Paying one's debts is a part of being honest.

> And again, verily I say unto you, concerning your debts—behold it is my will that you shall pay all your debts.
>
> And it is my will that you shall humble yourselves before me, and obtain this blessing by your diligence and humility and the prayer of faith.
>
> And inasmuch as you are diligent and humble, and exercise the prayer of faith, behold, I will soften the hearts of those to whom you are in debt, until I shall send means unto you for your deliverance. (D&C 104:78–80.)

President Brigham Young later said:

> Joseph was doing business in Kirtland, and it seemed as though all creation was upon him, to hamper him in every way, and they drove him from his business, and it left him so that some of his debts had to be settled afterwards; and I am thankful to say that they were settled up; still further, we have sent East to New York, to Ohio, and to every place where I had any idea that Joseph had ever done business, and inquired if there was a man left to whom Joseph Smith, jun., the Prophet, owed a dollar, or a sixpence. If there was we would pay it.[7]

"Joseph Smith and Oliver Cowdery Translating the Book of Mormon,"
by Earl Jones.
Used by permission of The Church of Jesus Christ of Latter-day Saints.

9

Kindness

The kindness of a man should never be forgotten.[1]

Nothing is so much calculated to lead people to forsake sin as to take them by the hand, and watch over them with tenderness. When persons manifest the least kindness and love to me, O what power it has over my mind.[2]

—Joseph Smith

"Is there no place for you, my boy?"

In every association with his fellow beings, Joseph was considerate and just. He was always willing to carry his part of the burden and to share in any suffering or deprivation inflicted upon his friends. He was gentle to children and universally won their love.

Zion's Camp, which made the long march from Kirtland to Missouri, consisted mostly of men; however, there was one young person, Lyman O. Littlefield, who was only thirteen. He remembers the Prophet in the following story:

The journey was extremely toilsome for all, and the physical suffering, coupled with the knowledge of the persecutions endured by our brethren whom we were traveling to succor, caused me to lapse one day into a state of melancholy. As the camp was making ready to depart I sat tired and brooding by the roadside. The Prophet was the busiest man of the camp; and yet when he saw me, he turned from the great press of other duties to say a word of comfort to a child. Placing his hand upon my head, he said, "Is there no place for you, my boy? If not, we must make one." This circumstance made an impression upon my mind which long lapse of time and cares of riper years have not effaced.[3]

"We have overcome the world by love"

The following was told by the Prophet's mother:

The mob had the *kindness* to allow us the privilege of bringing them [the bodies of Joseph and Hyrum] home and burying them in Nauvoo, notwithstanding the immense reward which was offered by the Missourians for Joseph's head. . . .

After the corpses were washed and dressed in their burial clothes, we were allowed to see them. I had for a long time braced every nerve, roused every energy of my soul and called upon God to strengthen me, but when I entered the room and saw my murdered sons extended both at once before my eyes and heard the sobs and groans of my family and cries of "Father! Husband! Brothers!" from the lips of their wives, children, brothers and sisters, it was too much; I sank back, crying to the Lord in the agony of my soul, "My God, my God, why hast thou forsaken this family!"

A voice replied, "I have taken them to myself, that they might have rest." . . .

Of her feelings after receiving this heavenly comfort, she penned this beautiful expression: "As I looked upon their peaceful, smiling countenances, I seemed almost to hear them say, 'Mother, weep not for us, we have overcome the world by love; we carried to them the gospel, that their souls might be saved; they slew us for our testimony, and thus placed us beyond their power; their ascendancy is for a moment, ours is an eternal triumph.'"[4]

"People, old or young, loved him and trusted him instinctively"

Joseph Smith had many detractors and enemies, yet his personality was so warm, radiant, forceful, and dominant that those who came to know him looked upon him as the dominant personality of their lives and the greatest person they had ever met. All classes of people related to him; the rough-and-ready Porter Rockwell, the practical and energetic Brigham Young, and the enlightened Eliza R. Snow, who lived in Joseph and Emma's home, taught their children, and was later sealed to Joseph.

William Taylor, who for a while had a close association with him, said of Joseph's personality:

> I have never known the same joy and satisfaction in the companionship of any other person, man or woman, that I felt with him, the man who had conversed with the Almighty. He was always the most companionable and lovable of men—cheerful and jovial. . . .
>
> Much has been said of his geniality and personal magnetism. I was a witness of this—people, old or young, loved him and trusted him instinctively. . . . My devotion to the prophet was akin to that felt by all who came under his influence.[5]

William M. Allred, who as a boy knew Joseph, said, concerning his appearance and character: "I thought he had a very noble appearance, very kind and affectionate."[6]

"My brother and I both got fast in the mud"

Margaret McIntyre Burgess, who as a child lived with her parents in Nauvoo, Illinois, related this incident as her cherished recollection of the Prophet Joseph.

> My older brother and I were going to school, near to the building which was known as Joseph's [brick] store. It had been raining the previous day, causing the ground to be very muddy, especially along that street. My brother Wallace and I both got fast in the mud and could not get out, and, of course, child-like, we began to cry, for we thought we would have to stay there.
>
> But looking up, I beheld the loving friend of children, the Prophet Joseph coming to us. He soon had us on higher and drier ground. Then he stooped down and cleaned the mud from our little, heavy-laden shoes, took his handkerchief from his pocket, and wiped our tear-stained faces. He

spoke kind and cheering words to us and sent us on our way to school rejoicing.[7]

"He lifted me upon his own broad shoulders . . . and saved my life"

The following story is adapted from the writings of John Lyman Smith, at the time Joseph's teenage cousin.

One evening in the summer of 1837, Joseph and I drove a carriage into the little town of Painesville, Ohio, and stopped at the house of a friend for supper. We had scarcely finished our meal when a disturbance arose outside. A mob had gathered; there were angry yells and threats of murder. They demanded that our host bring Joseph and me out to them. Instead, he led us out through a back door and helped us to get away in the darkness.

Pretty soon the mob discovered we had escaped, so they dispatched riders to hurry along the road they thought we would take. Bonfires were lighted, sentinels were placed, they hunted the countryside.

Joseph and I did not take the main road, however, but walked through the woods and swamps away from the road. We were helped by the bonfires. Pretty soon I began to falter in our flight. Sickness and fright had robbed me of strength.

Joseph had to decide whether to leave me to be captured by the mob or to endanger himself by rendering aid. Choosing the latter course, he lifted me upon his own broad shoulders and bore me with occasional rests through the swamp and darkness. Several hours later, we emerged upon the lonely road and soon reached safety. Joseph's herculean strength permitted him to accomplish this task and saved my life."[8]

"I have no shoes"
"Let them have boots, then"

Another experience is related by John Lyman Smith, Joseph's sixteen-year-old cousin, who on this occasion had been marching with seventy-five troopers of the Nauvoo Legion. In June 1844, only a few days before the Prophet was martyred in Carthage, they had been called up in case of any difficulties with the visit of Governor Ford to Carthage and Nauvoo.

It had been raining; the roads were bad. Most of the men had walked many miles on foot, wading in places through waist-deep water. They were tired and sore, but excited to see their Prophet. John tells of the kindness of their leader:

> We reached Nauvoo about daylight and encamped near the temple. While I was guarding the baggage, Joseph the Prophet rode up. He asked about my parents. As we were talking, he took my hand and pulled me forward until I was obliged to step up on a log. . . . Seeing that each foot left marks of blood upon the bark, he asked me what was the matter with my feet.
>
> I replied that the prairie grass had cut my shoes to pieces and wounded my feet, but they would soon be all right. I noticed the hand he raised to his face was wet and looking up I saw his cheeks covered with tears. He placed his hand on my head and said, "God bless you, my dear boy," and asked if others of the company were in the same plight. I replied that a number of them were.
>
> Turning his face toward Mr. Lathrup as the latter came to the door of his store, the Prophet said: "Let these men have some shoes." Lathrup said, "I have no shoes." Joseph's quick reply was, "Let them have boots, then."[9]

Within a few short days, the Prophet was martyred. The troops were never called upon to fight. In fact, the Prophet pleaded with Elder John Taylor before his death to not have the men fight. The Lord taught, "vengeance is mine, and I will repay" (Mormon 3:15).

But the men never forgot the love of their Prophet.

Joseph taught the brethren kindness to animals

The Apostle Paul, on one occasion, shook a venomous snake from his hand, and was not injured by it (Acts 28:3–6). No less remarkable is an incident from the famous march of Zion's Camp to help the Saints in Missouri.

The members of that organization sometimes encountered reptiles on the prairie. One day Solomon Humphreys lay down for a little rest, being weary. When he awoke, he saw a rattlesnake coiled up less than a foot from his head.

Some proposed to kill it, but Brother Humphreys said, "No, I'll protect him; you shan't hurt him, for he and I had a good nap together."

It was only a few days before this that the Prophet Joseph instructed the brethren not to kill serpents, or any other animals unless it was necessary in order to preserve themselves from hunger. "Men must become harmless, before the brute creation," he said.[10]

10

Leadership

A visitor, who remarked that the people had been gathered from the four quarters of the earth, of different races
and creeds, asked the Prophet:
  "Mr. Smith, how do you govern these people?"
  [The Prophet replied:] "I teach them correct principles
and they govern themselves!"[1]

—Joseph Smith

"I am determined while I do lead the Church, to lead it right"

On May 27, 1843, as Joseph was addressing the Twelve, he
paused and gave the following advice to those present: "The
Saints need not think that because I am familiar with them
and am playful and cheerful, that I am ignorant of what is
going on. Iniquity of any kind cannot be sustained in the
Church, and it will not fare well where I am; for I am determined while I do lead the Church, to lead it right.[2]

Instruction to women leaders

Joseph was straightforward in his teachings given to
women in the Church. On the afternoon of Thursday, April 28,
1842, he gave them advice at a Relief Society meeting:

He exhorted the sisters always to concentrate their faith
and prayers for, and place confidence in those whom God
has appointed to honor, whom God has plac'd at the head
to lead—that we should arm them with our prayers. . . .

You must put down iniquity and by your good example provoke the Elders to good works—if you do right [there is] no danger of going too fast; he said he did not care how fast we run in the path of virtue. Resist evil and there is no danger. . . .

It is natural for females to have feelings of charity—you are now placed in a situation where you can act according to those sympathies which God has planted in your bosoms. If you live up to these principles how great and glorious—if you live up to your privilege the angels cannot be restrain'd from being your associates. . . .

. . . Not war, not jangle, not contradiction, but meekness, love, purity, these are the things that should magnify us. . . .

Let this Society teach how to act towards husbands, to treat them with mildness and affection. When a man is borne down with trouble—when he is perplexed, if he can meet a smile, [not] an argument—if he can meet with mildness, it will calm down his soul and smooth his feelings. When the mind is going to despair it needs a solace. . . .

Don't envy sinners—have mercy on them, God will destroy them.[3]

"He was ever the leader"

In describing the leadership qualities of the Prophet he loved so much, George Q. Cannon said:

Whether engaging in manly sport, during hours of relaxation, or proclaiming words of wisdom in pulpit or grove, he was ever the leader. His magnetism was masterful, and his heroic qualities won universal admiration. Where he moved all classes were forced to recognize in him the man of power. Strangers journeying to see him from a distance, knew him the moment their eyes beheld his person. Men have crossed ocean and continent to meet him, and have selected him instantly from among a multitude.

. . . He performed a work, "not pagan ire, nor tooth of time, nor sword, nor fire, shall bring to naught."[4]

"The Lord sustains any man that holds a portion of the Priesthood"

Wilford Woodruff was a faithful participant in Zion's Camp and was later called by Joseph Smith to be an Apostle when he was only thirty-two years old. He served faithfully as an Apostle and then as President of the Church, for almost sixty years. He was one of the Church's most successful missionaries and a beloved friend of Joseph Smith.

He found it hard to understand and accept that some of the brethren lost faith and turned against the Church when they were not called to be leaders, and several of the leading brethren had to be excommunicated because of the pride in their hearts.

We have been warned:

> We have learned by sad experience that it is the nature and disposition of almost all men, as soon as they get a little authority, as they suppose, they will immediately begin to exercise unrighteous dominion.
>
> Hence many are called, but few are chosen.
>
> No power or influence can or ought to be maintained by virtue of the priesthood. (D&C 121:39–41.)

In response to their loss of spiritual humility, Wilford Woodruff, who as a priest had been sent on a mission by Joseph, said:

> I traveled thousands of miles and preached the Gospel as a Priest, and . . . the Lord sustained me and made manifest His power in the defense of my life as much while I held that office as He has done while I have held the office of an Apostle. The Lord sustains any man that holds a portion of the Priesthood, whether he is a Priest, an Elder, a Seventy, or an Apostle, if he magnifies his calling and does his duty.[5]

The mantle of Joseph rested upon Brigham

When the Lord gives greater responsibility to a person, the person often rises to the occasion and performs his calling better than anyone ever thought he could. People say leaders change when the "mantle" of the calling falls upon them. Never was this more vividly shown than after Joseph was martyred and the Church leaders met to determine who would be the next leader.

Most of the members of the Quorum of the Twelve were not in Nauvoo at the time of the martyrdom. They were scattered about the East preaching the gospel. Some seemed to sense a gloom come over them a few days before the mob rushed the Carthage Jail on June 27, 1844. Several had already begun the journey home before they found out about Joseph and Hyrum's deaths. By August 7, 1844, most of the Twelve had arrived back in Nauvoo.

Even though Joseph had explained to the Quorum of the Twelve how the priesthood power would be held by the quorum until a new leader was named, most of the Church members were not aware of the promised line of succession, and some felt the leadership should fall upon the shoulders of Sidney Rigdon, Joseph's first counselor. Sidney, a former Campbellite minister, was a great orator and had been used many times as a spokesman for the Prophet Joseph Smith.

On August 7, 1844, a meeting was held among the Church authorities. During this meeting, Sidney Rigdon said: "I have been ordained a spokesman to Joseph, and I must come to Nauvoo and see that the church is governed in a proper manner. . . ." Brigham Young announced a special conference the next day at ten o'clock.[6]

A large congregation of Saints gathered for the next morning's meeting. Sidney Rigdon talked to them for an hour and a half, advancing his claim as "guardian for the Church." Then Brigham Young arose to tell the Saints that a second session would be held in the afternoon at two o'clock.[7]

At that afternoon meeting a most unusual thing happened. As President Young stood to speak, the mantle of the Prophet Joseph rested visibly upon him.

Benjamin Johnson described the event as follows: "In every possible degree it was Joseph's voice, and his person, in look, attitude, dress and appearance was Joseph himself, personified; and I knew in a moment the spirit and mantle of Joseph was upon [Brigham]."[8]

George Q. Cannon, then a boy in his teens, later testified, "If Joseph had risen from the dead and again spoken in their hearing, the effect could not have been more startling."[9]

Zina Huntington wrote: "All witnessed the transfiguration. . . .
I closed my eyes. I could have exclaimed, 'I know that is Joseph
Smith's voice!' Yet I knew he had gone. But the same spirit was
with the people."[10]
Wilford Woodruff said:

> I was there, the Twelve were there, and a good many others,
> and all can bear the same testimony. . . . Here was Sidney
> Rigdon and other men rising up and claiming to be the
> leaders of the Church, and men stood, as it were, on a
> pivot, not knowing which way to turn. But just as quick as
> Brigham Young rose in that assembly, his face was that of
> Joseph Smith—the mantle of Joseph had fallen upon him,
> the power of God that was upon Joseph Smith was upon
> him, he had the voice of Joseph, and it was the voice of the
> shepherd. . . . There was a reason for this in the mind of
> God; it convinced the people.[11]

Brigham Young spoke to the congregation with great power,
saying:

> *Attention all! . . .*
> For the first time in the kingdom of God in the 19th
> century, without a Prophet at our head, do I step forth to
> act in my calling in connection with the Quorum of the
> Twelve . . . Apostles whom God has called by revelation
> through the Prophet Joseph, who are ordained and
> anointed to bear off the keys of the kingdom of God in all
> the world. . . .
> They stand next to Joseph, and are as the First
> Presidency of the Church. . . .
> You cannot fill the office of a prophet, seer and revelator:
> God must do this. You are like children without a father and
> sheep without a shepherd. You must not appoint any man
> at our head; if you should, the Twelve must ordain him. . . .
> You cannot take Elder Rigdon and place him above the
> Twelve. . . .
> Do you want the church properly organized, or do you
> want a spokesman to be chief cook and bottle-washer? . . .
> Now, if you want Sidney Rigdon or William Law to lead
> you, or anybody else, you are welcome to them; but I tell
> you, in the name of the Lord. . . .

We have a head, and that head is the Apostleship. . . .

All that want to draw away a party from the church after them, let them do it if they can, but they will not pros-´ per.

Several others spoke briefly, then Brigham stood again and put the matter to a vote, saying:

Here are the Apostles, the *Bible,* the *Book of Mormon,* the *Doctrine and Covenants*—they are written on the tablet of my heart. If the church want the Twelve to stand as the head, the First Presidency of the Church, and at the head of this kingdom in all the world. . . . All that are in favor of this, in all the congregation of the Saints, manifest it by holding up the right hand.

The vote was unanimous. When the Saints were asked if there was a contrary mind, not a single hand was raised. Not even that of Sidney Rigdon or those who supported him. The Lord had spoken; Brigham Young had the mantle of Joseph and was the prophet, seer, and revelator for The Church of Jesus Christ of Latter-day Saints, to stand as Joseph had stood, to be the spokesman for the Lord.[12]

"They could not destroy the appointment of the Prophet of God"

Occasionally, there are those who feel that they should not follow the leadership of the Church. They feel uncomfortable with the bishop or stake president they are asked to follow. This also happened in the time of Joseph Smith. We can learn a great lesson from this experience.

In Kirtland, Joseph and several of the brethren formed the Kirtland Safety Society. This organization issued its own paper money and guaranteed payment. Kirtland residents joined in the spirit of speculation that swept the United States, and when the boom burst, many banks failed, suspending all payments to depositors. The Kirtland bank was one of those that suffered in the crash. Those who lost funds were very bitter about the situation.

Some who were not strong in the faith apostatized from the

Church, saying that a true prophet could not be involved in a bank failure. They felt that the Lord should have told Joseph ahead of time, so that their funds could have been withdrawn. They failed to separate his religious and prophetic powers from his role in secular affairs, wherein of course it was possible for him to be unsuccessful. Several elders of the Church called a meeting at the Kirtland Temple, where the issue under discussion was how the Prophet Joseph Smith could be deposed. Brigham Young attended the meeting and spoke in behalf of Joseph. He later recalled:

> I rose up, and in a plain and forcible manner told them that Joseph was a Prophet, and I knew it, and that they might rail and slander him as much as they pleased; they could not destroy the appointment of the Prophet of God, they could only destroy their own authority, cut the thread that bound them to the Prophet and to God, and sink themselves to hell.[13]

Several years later, President Wilford Woodruff further clarified this very important principle of the gospel. The prophet is called by God and released by God. He cannot outlive his calling, nor can he lead the Saints astray.

> The Lord will never permit me or any other man who stands as President of this Church to lead you astray. It is not in the programme. It is not in the mind of God. If I were to attempt that, the Lord would remove me out of my place, and so He will any other man who attempts to lead the children of men astray from the oracles of God and from their duty. (Doctrine and Covenants, p. 292.)

Joseph's vision of the Salt Lake Valley

Great leaders must be visionary people, who can see beyond the struggles of today's problems to the solutions of the future. Joseph realized the need for the Saints to find a place where they could raise up a righteous generation of followers without the persecution they had faced in New York, Ohio, Missouri, and Illinois. Shortly before his martyrdom, the Lord blessed Joseph with a beautiful vision of the mountain valleys in the West to which his people would go. There they would prepare themselves for the great missionary journeys that would prepare the world for the second coming of our Lord and Savior, Jesus Christ.

Anson Call, who was present during the vision, recorded:

> I had before seen him in a vision, and now saw while he was talking his countenance change to white; not the deadly white of a bloodless face, but a living brilliant white. He seemed absorbed in gazing at something at a great distance, and said: "I am gazing upon the valleys of those mountains." This was followed by a vivid description of the scenery of these mountains, as I have since become acquainted with it. . . .
>
> It is impossible to represent in words this scene which is still vivid in my mind, of the grandeur of Joseph's appearance, his beautiful descriptions of this land, and his wonderful prophetic utterances as they emanated from the glorious inspiration that overshadowed him. There was a force and power in his exclamations of which the following is but a faint echo. "Oh, the beauty of those snow-capped mountains! The cool refreshing streams that are running down through those mountain gorges!" Then gazing in another direction, as if there was a change of locality: "Oh, the scenes that this people will pass through! The dead that will lay between here and there." Then turning in another direction as if the scene had again changed: "Oh, the apostasy that will take place before my brethren reach that land."[14]

Joseph Smith's "American religion"

Count Leo Tolstoi, the great Russian author of *War and Peace,* statesman, and philosopher, had an interesting opinion as to the destiny of the "American Religion" founded by Joseph Smith. The following experience was told to Thomas J. Yates, a Cornell University student, by Dr. Andrew D. White, former president of Cornell University and former U.S. Foreign Minister to Russia. It occurred in 1892, while Dr. White and Count Tolstoi were discussing religion.

"Dr. White," said Count Tolstoi, "I wish you would tell me about your American religion."

"We have no state church in America," replied Dr. White.

"I know that, but what about your American religion?"

Patiently then Dr. White explained to the count that in America there are many religions, and that each person is free to belong to the particular church in which he is interested.

To this Tolstoi impatiently replied: "I know all of this, but I want to know about the *American* religion. Catholicism originated in Rome; the Episcopal Church originated in England; the Lutheran Church in Germany, but the Church to which I refer originated in America, and is commonly known as the Mormon Church. What can you tell me about the teachings of the Mormons?"

"Well," said Dr. White, "I know very little concerning them. They have an unsavory reputation, they practice polygamy, and are very superstitious."

Then Count Leo Tolstoi in his honest and stern, but lovable, manner, rebuked the ambassador. "Dr. White, I am greatly surprised and disappointed that a man of your great learning and position should be so ignorant on this important subject. The Mormon people teach the American religion; their principles teach the people not only of Heaven and its attendant glories, but how to live so that their social and economic relations with each other are placed on a sound basis. If the people follow the teachings of this Church, nothing can stop their progress—it will be limitless. There have been great movements started in the past but they have died or been modified before they reached maturity. If Mormonism is able to endure, unmodified, until it reaches the third and fourth generation, it is destined to become the greatest power the world has ever known."[15]

Preach Jesus Christ and him crucified

On May 8, 1838, Joseph Smith was desirous of setting forth the answers to questions which had been presented to him over and over again. To one of these questions he replied as follows:

Question: "What are the fundamental principles of your religion?"

Answer: "The fundamental principles of our religion are the testimony of the Apostles and Prophets, concerning Jesus Christ, that He died, was buried, and rose again the third day, and ascended into heaven; and all other things which pertain to our religion are only appendages to it."[16]

On another occasion Joseph made a great promise to those who will be called upon to lead the restored Church of Jesus Christ. He clearly states what is our first responsibility: "Go in all meekness and sobriety, and preach Jesus Christ and Him crucified; not to contend with others on account of their faith, or systems of religion, but pursue a steady course. This I deliver by way of commandment, and all who observe it not will pull down persecution upon their heads, while those who do [obey it] shall always be filled with the Holy Ghost; this I pronounce as a prophecy."[17]

As Wilford Woodruff said: "There was never a set of men, since God made the world, under a stronger responsibility to warn this generation. We are required to do this. This is our calling. It is our duty. It is our business."[18]

11

Missionary Work

*Our missionaries are going forth to different nations . . .
the Standard of Truth has been erected; no unhallowed
hand can stop the work from progressing; persecutions
may rage, mobs may combine, armies may assemble,
calumny may defame, but the truth of God will go forth
boldly, nobly, and independent, till it has penetrated
every continent, visited every clime, swept every country,
and sounded in every ear, till the purposes of God shall be
accomplished, and the great Jehovah shall say the work
is done!*[1]

—Joseph Smith

"Are you good at a race?"

One of the Prophet's closest and most valiant friends was
Parley P. Pratt. He was ordained an Apostle at age twenty-
seven and went on many missionary journeys. Many of the
early converts to the Church first heard the restored gospel and
the testimony of the Sacred Grove from Parley. He lost his life
to an assassin's bullet while in the service of his Lord.

Of one of his missionary experiences in Ohio, he wrote that
he and his companions

> found the people all excited with the news of the great work
> we had been the humble instruments of doing in Kirtland
> and vicinity. Some wished to learn and obey the fulness of
> the gospel—were ready to entertain us and hear us preach.
> Others were filled with envy, rage and lying.
>
> We had stopped for the night at the house of Simeon
> Carter, by whom we were kindly received, and were in the
> act of reading to him and explaining the Book of Mormon,

when there came a knock at the door, and an officer entered with a warrant from a magistrate by the name of Byington, to arrest me on a very frivolous charge.

I dropped the Book of Mormon in Carter's house and went with [the officer]. . . .

[At the "trial"] I was soon ordered to prison, or to pay a sum of money which I had not in the world. . . . In the morning the officer appeared and took me to breakfast; this over, we sat waiting in the inn for all things to be ready to conduct me to prison. In the meantime my fellow travelers came past on their journey, and called to see me. I told them in an undertone to pursue their journey and leave me to manage my own affairs, promising to overtake them soon. They did so.

After sitting awhile by the fire in charge of the officer, I requested to step out. I walked out into the public square accompanied by him. Said I, "Mr. Peabody, are you good at a race?" "No," said he, "but my big bull dog is, and he has been trained to assist me in my office these several years; he will take any man down at my bidding."

"Well, Mr. Peabody, you compelled me to go a mile, I have gone with you two miles. You have given me an opportunity to preach, sing, and have also entertained me with lodging and breakfast. I must now go on my journey; if you are good at a race you can accompany me. I thank you for all your kindness—good day, sir."

I then started on my journey, while he stood amazed and not able to step one foot before the other. Seeing this, I halted, turned to him and again invited him to a race. He still stood amazed. I then renewed my exertions, and soon increased my speed to something like that of a deer.

He did not awake from his astonishment sufficiently to start in pursuit till I had gained, perhaps, two hundred yards. I had already leaped a fence, and was making my way through a field to the forest on the right of the road. He now came hallooing after me, and shouting to his dog to seize me. The dog, being one of the largest I ever saw, came close on my footsteps with all his fury; the officer behind still in pursuit, clapping his hands and hallooing, "stu-boy, stu-boy—take him—watch—lay hold of him, I say—down with him," and pointing his finger in the direction I was running.

The dog was fast overtaking me, and in the act of leaping upon me, when, quick as lightning, the thought struck me, to assist the officer, in sending the dog with all fury to the forest a little distance before me. I pointed my finger in that direction, clapped my hands, and shouted in imitation of the officer. The dog hastened past me with redoubled speed towards the forest; being urged by the officer and myself, and both of us running in the same direction.

Gaining the forest, I soon lost sight of the officer and dog, and have not seen them since.[2]

"Parley's escape was successful. The officer later returned to Simeon Carter's home, retrieved the copy of the Book of Mormon that Parley had dropped, studied it, went to Kirtland, and was baptized. The officer returned to his home and 'commenced to preach and baptize.' A church of about sixty members was soon organized in the place where Parley had played the trick of deception on the dog."[3]

"It shall be given you in the very hour, yea, in the very moment, what ye shall say"

During a missionary journey to the Eastern States and Canada, Joseph Smith received the revelation now known as section 100 of the Doctrine and Covenants. In the revelation the Lord challenged him and his companions: "lift up your voices unto this people; speak the thoughts that I shall put in your hearts, and you shall not be confounded before men; for it shall be given you in the very hour, yea, in the very moment, what ye shall say" (D&C 100:5–6).

When the Prophet's party arrived in Mount Pleasant, Canada, Freeman Nickerson introduced them to his two wealthy sons, Moses and Freeman. The latter told his father: "Well father, I will welcome them for your sake, but I would just about as soon you had brought a nest of vipers and turned them loose upon us.". . .

"Oh," said he [the son], "just let him talk; I'll silence him if he undertakes to talk about the Bible. I guess I know as much about the scriptures as he does."

This was to his wife whom he directed to place the family Bible on the table in the parlor.

As soon as supper was over, he invited his visitors and family to go upstairs to the parlor, where he said . . . to the Prophet:

"Now, Mr. Smith, I wish you and Mr. Rigdon to speak freely. Say what you wish and tell us what you believe. We will listen."

Turning to his wife, he whispered, "Now you'll see how I shall shut him up."

The Prophet commenced by relating the scenes of his early life. He told how the angel visited him, of his finding the plates, the translation of them, and gave a short account of the matter contained in the Book of Mormon.

As the speaker continued his wonderful narrative, Lydia, [a house guest of the Nickerson family's] who was listening and watching him intently, saw his face become white and a shining glow seemed to beam from every feature.

As his story progressed he would often allude to passages of scripture. Then Mr. Nickerson would speak up and endeavor to confound him. But the attempt was soon acknowledged even by himself to be futile.

The Prophet bore a faithful testimony that the Priesthood was again restored to the earth, and that God and His Son had conferred upon him the keys of the Aaronic and Melchizedek Priesthoods. He stated that the last dispensation had come and the words of Jesus were now in force— "Go ye into all the world and preach the gospel to every creature. He that believeth and is baptized shall be saved; but he that believeth not shall be damned." (Mark 16: 15–16.)

Following this, Elder Rigdon spoke; whereupon, Mr. Nickerson said: "And is this then the curious religion the newspapers tell so much about? Why if what you have just said is not good sound sense, then I don't know what sense is."

Within a few days, Lydia and Mr. Nickerson and all of his household [twelve people in all] were baptized.[4]

Most of the Twelve leave for missions in Great Britain

Just a few short months after Joseph and his companions escaped from Liberty Jail, the Lord told him to call most of the Twelve Apostles to serve missions in Great Britain. With a couple of exceptions, the bond between the Prophet and the Twelve was strong. They accepted his every word as prophecy. They loved him, and even though they were sick and their families destitute, they accepted the Lord's call to serve.

Elders John Taylor and Wilford Woodruff were the first, leaving on the 8th day of August 1839. Elder Woodruff arose from the bed to which he had been confined for two weeks in order to start on this journey. Both of these devoted men left their no less devoted families at Montrose in sickness and poverty and distress; and yet all relying upon the Lord for preservation and blessing. . . .

Elders Brigham Young and Heber C. Kimball started together on the 18th of September, 1839. Brigham was so sick that he was unable to walk a few rods down to the river without assistance. He left his wife ill with a babe only ten days old, and all his other children helpless. Heber was in the same plight. His wife and all her children but one were prostrated."[5]

Heber recorded in his journal: I "said to Brother Brigham, 'This is pretty tough, isn't it; let's rise up and give them a cheer.' We arose, and swinging our hats three times over our heads, shouted: 'Hurrah, hurrah for Israel.' . . . Vilate and Mary Ann Young cried out to us: 'Goodbye, God bless you.' "[6]

After Brigham and Heber had traveled thirteen miles on their journey, they stopped at the residence of a friend and were so feeble as to be unable to carry into the house their trunks, which contained the very few articles of clothing they were able to take with them. In less than a month after their departure President Brigham Young's father, John Young, died.[7]

But miracles also happened to these dedicated Apostles. En route to the east, they often took a coach. Every time Brigham reached inside the trunk for the fare money, he found just enough. He assumed Heber had replenished their cash supplies; however, he later learned that Heber had not because he too was broke. The $13.50 donation they had been given in Nauvoo paid $87.00 worth of coach fares. They could only assume the money had been given them by an unseen hand eager to have the gospel of Jesus Christ move forward.[8]

On the 21st of September, 1839, Elder George A. Smith departed for England. He left his father, mother, sister and brother sick in a log stable, all unable to help themselves or each other. He, himself, was so emaciated that after he was a little way on his journey, he met some men who cried out: "Somebody has been robbing a graveyard of a skeleton.". . .

. . . The Prophet said of [these missionaries to England]: "Perhaps no men ever undertook such an important mission under such peculiarly distressing, forbidding and unpropitious circumstances. Most of them . . . were worn down with sickness and disease or were taken sick on the road. Several of their families were also afflicted and needed their aid and support. But knowing that they had been called by the God of heaven to preach the gospel to other nations, they conferred not with flesh and blood, but obedient to the heavenly mandate, without purse or scrip, commenced a journey of five thousand miles entirely dependent on the providence of that God who had called them to such a holy calling."[9]

Apostles return from their missions

On Thursday, July 1st, 1841, a river boat, coming up the Mississippi from St. Louis, stopped at the wharf in Nauvoo. A crowd had gathered to meet this boat, as three well known members of the Church, Brigham Young, Heber C. Kimball and John Taylor, were arriving home after their successful missions to England.

"When we landed in Nauvoo on the 1st of July," wrote Heber C. Kimball, "and when we struck the dock, I think there were about 300 Saints there to meet us, and a greater manifestation of love and gladness, I never saw before. President Smith was the first one that caught us by the hand. I never saw him feel better in my life than he does at this time; this is the case with the Saints in general."

Joseph was no doubt greatly pleased to welcome these faithful brethren of the Twelve, on their return from England. They, with five of their companions, Parley P. Pratt, Orson Pratt, Wilford Woodruff, George A. Smith and Willard Richards, had performed a missionary work in one year in the British Isles, which [to this time, 1944] has not been equaled in the history of the Church.

Of their great success, Brigham Young had written on leaving Liverpool:

"It was with a heart full of thanksgiving and gratitude to God, my heavenly Father, that I reflected upon his dealings with me and my brethren of the Twelve, during the past year of my life, which was spent in England. It truly seemed a miracle to look upon the contrast between our landing and departing from Liverpool. We landed in the spring of 1840, as strangers in a strange land and penniless, but through the mercy of God we have gained many friends, established churches in almost every noted town and city in the kingdom of Great Britain, baptized between seven and eight thousand, printed 5,000 Books of Mormon, 3,000 Hymn Books, 2,500 volumes of the *Millennial Star*, and 50,000 tracts, and emigrated to Zion 1,000 souls, established a permanent shipping agency, which will be a great blessing to the Saints, and have left sown in the hearts of many thousands the seeds of eternal truth, which will bring forth fruit to the honor and glory of God, and yet we have lacked nothing to eat, drink or wear; in all these things I acknowledge the hand of God."[10]

"Joseph Smith went into the river and baptized eighty persons"

In the Sunday meeting, held on March 20, 1842, Wilford Woodruff tells us:

President Smith said he should attend to the ordinance of baptism in the river, near his house, at two o'clock, and at the appointed hour, the bank of the Mississippi was lined with a multitude of people, and President Joseph Smith went into the river and baptized eighty persons for the remission of their sins, and what added joy to the scene was, that the first person baptized was M. L. D. Wasson, a nephew of Mrs. Emma Smith—the first of her kindred that has embraced the fullness of the Gospel.

At the close of this interesting scene, the administrator lifted up his hands towards heaven, and implored the blessing of God to rest upon the people; and truly the Spirit of God did rest upon the multitude, to the joy and consolation of our hearts.

After baptism, the congregation again repaired to the grove . . . and, notwithstanding President Smith had spoken in the open air to the people, and stood in the water and baptized about eighty persons, about fifty of those baptized received their confirmation under his hands in the after part of the day.[11]

"By small means the Lord can bring about great things"

Samuel Smith, younger brother of Joseph, was among the first missionaries of the Church after its organization, traveling without purse or scrip to the surrounding communities. His mission was to sell copies of the Book of Mormon and preach the restored gospel of Jesus Christ.

Seeking shelter at night under trees or in barns, relying on the hospitality of strangers for food, Samuel worked his way through the countryside with limited success. Finally, however, he found one circuit preacher, John Greene, who agreed to retain the book to sell to any interested parties he found.

Samuel Smith returned five times to retrieve the book from the Greenes, and on the last visit, John's wife, Rhoda, confessed she had secretly read the book and knew it was true. The Spirit told Samuel to leave that book with her.

About the same time, Rhoda's brother, Phineas H. Young, obtained a book from Samuel. Phineas shared it with his brother, Brigham, and also with his sister, Fanny Young Murray. Fanny shared it with her daughter, Vilate Kimball, who in turn shared it with her husband, Heber C. Kimball. John Greene also read it. After thorough study of the book, Brigham Young said, "I knew it was true, as well as I knew that I could see with my eyes."

From this one effort, numerous people were converted and came into the Church, one of whom would later succeed Joseph at his death and lead the Church for thirty-three years. "And thus we see that by small means the Lord can bring about great things" (1 Nephi 16:29).[12]

"I professed to be nothing but a man, a minister of salvation"

Referring to Oliver Cowdery, the Lord commanded: "At all times, and in all places, he shall open his mouth and declare my gospel as with the voice of a trump" (D&C 24:12). The Lord's further words, directed then to missionaries, clearly are applicable to all Latter-day Saints: "With some I am not well pleased, for they will not open their mouths, but they hide the talent which I have given unto them, because of the fear of man. Wo unto such, for my anger is kindled against them." (D&C 60:2.)

The Lord must have been pleased with the following missionary experience of the Prophet Joseph:

Saturday, November 3, 1839, Joseph found himself in very difficult circumstances. He and several friends were "the royal prisoners" of two competing generals. "[General] Clark wanted the privilege of putting us to death himself, and [General] Lucas, and his troops were desirous of exhibiting us in the streets of Independence."

While the generals were having their little power struggle, Joseph was ever the missionary.

Sunday, 4.—We were visited by some ladies and gentlemen. One of the women came up, and very candidly inquired of the troops which of the prisoners was the Lord whom the "Mormons" worshiped? One of the guard pointed to me with a significant smile, and said, "This is he." The woman then turning to me inquired whether I professed to be the Lord and Savior? I replied, that I professed to be nothing but a man, and a minister of salvation, sent by Jesus Christ to preach the Gospel.

This answer so surprised the woman that she began to

inquire into our doctrine, and I preached a discourse, both to her and her companions, and to the wondering soldiers, who listened with almost breathless attention while I set forth the doctrine of faith in Jesus Christ, and repentance, and baptism for remission of sins, with the promise of the Holy Ghost, as recorded in the second chapter of the Acts of the Apostles.

The woman was satisfied, and praised God in the hearing of the soldiers, and went away, praying that God would protect and deliver us. Thus was fulfilled a prophecy which had been spoken publicly by me, a few months previous— that a sermon should be preached in Jackson county by one of our Elders, before the close of 1838.[13]

Joseph never passed up the opportunity to "open his mouth," and sometimes his bravery and candor may have helped save his life.

"Preaching tenderly from between the iron bars . . . the gospel of peace to those who wanted to kill them"

Joseph taught the gospel of repentance until the very end of his life. Dan Jones, a fellow prisoner at Carthage Jail, whom the Prophet sent on an errand before the mob attacked, reported:

> The jail was watched by eight or ten of Captain Dunn's escort, and these were the least prejudiced of any; and due to the efforts of the prisoners and the rest of us in preaching to them, they believed our testimony to the point of confessing that the accusations made by the mobbers were lies for the purpose of getting revenge on J. Smith. Not infrequently they were heard persuading this one and that one to return to their homes and not to join with the mobs to persecute any further.

Two days after the martyrdom, Brother Jones attended a viewing of the bodies of Joseph and Hyrum, as the Saints paid their last respects to their beloved prophet. He later wrote that he then beheld "the two wisest and most virtuous men on the earth without any doubt, whom I had seen just awhile before preaching tenderly from between the iron bars of their jail the gospel of peace to those who wanted to kill them."[14]

The night before the martyrdom, after the others had fallen asleep, Joseph asked Elder Jones: "Are you afraid to die?" The short, sturdy Welshman responded: "Has that time come, think you? Engaged in such a cause, I do not think that death would have many terrors." The Prophet Joseph then spoke perhaps his last words of prophecy in mortality: "You will yet see Wales, and fulfill the mission appointed you before you die."[15]

The next day, Joseph sent Dan Jones to deliver a letter to O. H. Browning, asking him to represent the Prophet and Hyrum in the forthcoming trial. Joseph and Hyrum were murdered while he was on his errand.

Several months later, he was called to serve a mission with his wife in his native Wales. He preached and presided over the mission for several years in the 1840s and 1850s. On his first mission about 3,600 people were baptized; on his second, more than 2,000 additional converts joined the Church. Most of these converts made the trek across the plains to Utah.

President Gordon B. Hinckley said, "The entire Church needs to be told of this stocky little Welshman who, in terms of the number of converts, must certainly be included in the half dozen or so most productive missionaries in the history of the Church."[16]

Dan Jones had a great example to follow—his friend and Prophet, Joseph Smith, who taught "tenderly from between the iron bars . . . the gospel of peace to those who wanted to kill him."

Financial support for missionaries

Speaking of financial support of the early missionaries of the Church, Brigham Young said:

> I came into this Church in the spring of 1832. Previous to my being baptized, I took a mission to Canada at my own expense; and from the time that I was baptized until the day of . . . the martyrdom of Joseph and Hyrum, no summer passed over my head but what I was traveling and preaching, and the only thing I ever received from the

Church, during over twelve years, and the only means that were ever given me by the Prophet, that I now recollect, was in 1842, when brother Joseph sent me the half of a small pig that the brethren had brought to him. . . .

And that fall, . . . brother Heber [C. Kimball] was credited two dollars in the Church books for one day's services, by brother Willard Richards who was then keeping those books. Brother Heber said, "Blot that out, for I don't want it." . . . I have traveled and preached, and at the same time sustained my family by my labor and economy.[17]

Brigham Young further stated that it was never hard for him to travel without purse or scrip. As an example he related his experience in England in 1839.

He and his companions had left home, sick and without money. Some time after their arrival in Preston, they decided to begin the publication of a magazine, under the name of the Millennial Star, with Parley P. Pratt as editor. The "Star" was printed and paid for with borrowed money. Three thousand hymnbooks, five thousand copies of the Book of Mormon, and thousands of tracts were also printed.

Brigham Young remained in England a few days over a year. During that time he paid expenses incurred by the establishment of the Church in London, in addition to the printing. When he left, he had paid the debt and had money to pay for the passage home. "And that," he said, "though I had not a sixpence when we first landed in Preston, and I do not know that one of the Twelve had."[18]

12

Obedience

---

*This is the word of the Lord to us, and . . . we will obey:
as on conditions of our obedience He has promised us
great things; yea, even a visit from the heavens to honor
us with His own presence. We greatly fear before the Lord
lest we should fail of this great honor, which our Master
proposes to confer on us; we are seeking for humility and
great faith lest we be ashamed in His presence.*[1]

—Joseph Smith

"When the Lord commands, do it"

Joseph, especially after the experience of losing the first
116 pages of the Book of Mormon manuscript, was very diligent in doing what the Lord commanded. He realized that he,
like Solomon of old, had been commanded of the Lord to build
a temple: "Take heed now; for the Lord hath chosen thee to
build an house for the sanctuary; be strong and do it. . . . And
David said to Solomon his son, Be strong and of good courage,
and do it; fear not, nor be dismayed; for the Lord God, even my
God, will be with thee; he will not fail thee, nor forsake thee,
until thou hast finished all the work for the service of the
house of the Lord." (1 Chronicles 28:10, 20.)

Joseph knew that many of the people were in very poor financial situations, but he lived by faith and tried to obey every
word that proceeded from the mouth of God. He recorded: "No
month ever found me more busily engaged . . . but as my life
consisted of activity and unyielding exertions, I made this my
rule: *When the Lord commands, do it.*"[2]

"He who is faithful and wise in time is accounted worthy to inherit the mansions . . . of my Father"

In December, 1831, less than two years after the Church was organized with only six members, Joseph was told by the Lord to call Newel K. Whitney as bishop in Kirtland (D&C 72:7–8). At that time revelation was given through Joseph Smith outlining eternally sound leadership principles. This is a great testimony to the truthfulness of The Church of Jesus Christ of Latter-day Saints, for the principles taught came from Jesus Christ through revelation, not from the young prophet: "It is required of the Lord, at the hand of every steward, to render an account of his stewardship, both in time and in eternity. For he who is faithful and wise in time is accounted worthy to inherit the mansions prepared for him of my Father." (D&C 72:3–4.)

Brigham Young added in his frank, straightforward way an insight on this theme:

> We are trying to teach this people to use their brains, that they may obtain knowledge and wisdom to sustain themselves and to dictate for others; that they may be worthy to be made kings and priests to God, which they never can be unless they learn, here or somewhere else, to govern, manage, legislate, and sustain themselves, their families, and friends, even to the making of nations, and nation after nation. If they cannot attain to this, they will have to be servants somewhere.[3]

Joseph, in explaining how God, our Eternal Father, became God, added:

> God himself was once as we are now, and is an exalted man, and sits enthroned in yonder heavens! That is the great secret. . . . We have imagined and supposed that God was God from all eternity. I will refute that idea, and take away the veil, so that you may see.[4]

What is the great promise made to every priesthood holder? It is known as the oath and covenant of the priesthood (see D&C 84:33–44), which promises:

Whoso is faithful unto the obtaining of these two priest-hoods [Aaronic and Melchizedek] . . . and the magnifying their calling, are sanctified. . . .

And also all they who receive this priesthood receive me, saith the Lord;

For he that receiveth my servants receiveth me;

And he that receiveth me receiveth my Father;

And he that receiveth my Father receiveth my Father's kingdom; therefore all that my Father hath shall be given unto him. . . .

Therefore, all those who receive the priesthood, receive this oath and covenant of my Father, which he cannot break, neither can it be moved.

But whoso breaketh this covenant after he hath received it, and altogether turneth therefrom, shall not have forgiveness of sins in this world nor in the world to come. (D&C 84:33, 35–38, 40–41.)

Thomas B. Marsh and the strippings of milk

Through the Prophet Joseph the Lord commended Thomas B. Marsh for his obedience and faithfulness. But he then warned Thomas to be "patient in afflictions. . . . Govern your house in meekness, and be steadfast. . . . Pray always, lest you enter into temptation and lose your reward. Be faithful unto the end, and lo, I am with you . . . even Jesus Christ, your Redeemer." (D&C 31:9, 11–13.)

Thomas Marsh was being prepared as a leader; however, he utterly failed to obey the instruction to govern his house in humility and listen to the counsel of the Prophet Joseph. Elder George A. Smith told the story:

When the Saints were living in Far West, Missouri, Thomas Marsh's wife and Sister Harris agreed to exchange milk, in order to enable each of them to make more cheese than they could do separately. It was agreed that they should not save the "strippings" (the last milk drawn at a milking), that milk and strippings should all go together. Mrs. Harris performed her part of the agreement, but Mrs. Marsh kept a pint of strippings from each cow so as to make some really good cheese.

When this matter became known an appeal was taken to the bishop. He sustained Mrs. Harris. If Brother Marsh had obeyed the revelation (D&C 31) and governed his house in humility and with steadfastness, he would have righted the wrong done, but instead of doing so he appealed to the high council. Brother Marsh, who at the time was President of the Twelve, possibly thought that the council would favor him, but that body confirmed the bishop's decision.

He was not yet satisfied. He appealed to Joseph Smith and the First Presidency, who consented to review the case. Joseph and his two counselors considered the case, then approved the high council's decision. Was Brother Marsh satisfied then? No. With stubborn persistency he declared that he would uphold the character of his wife, "even if he had to go to hell for it."

Elder George A. Smith observed that Brother Marsh, who as President of the Twelve should have been the first to repent and do justice by returning the few "pints of milk strippings," became so angry that "he went before a magistrate and swore that the 'Mormons' were hostile towards the State of Missouri. That affidavit brought from [Governor Lilburn W. Boggs and] the government of Missouri an extermination order, which drove some 15,000 Saints from their homes . . . and some thousands perished through suffering the exposure consequent on this state of affairs."[5]

Governor Lilburn W. Boggs's Extermination Order read as follows:

> The Mormons must be treated as enemies and must be exterminated or driven from the state, if necessary for the public good.[6]

Thomas Marsh and a few other apostates helped the Saints' persecutors to justify their cruelties. Extermination began just three days after the governor's order. At Haun's Mill, a small Mormon settlement, nineteen people were massacred by several hundred men, who shot mercilessly through the cracks in the walls, killing and wounding fathers, sons, and children as their wives hid in the trees by the river.

In 1857, after many years of apostasy and suffering, Thomas B. Marsh went to Salt Lake to confess his sins and ask for pardon. He was a poor, discouraged man who knew he was responsible for the suffering of many people. He said: "I became jealous of the Prophet, and then I saw double, and overlooked everything that was right, and spent all my time in looking for the evil."[7]

At the time Brother Marsh was reinstated as a member of the Church, President Brigham Young referred to the fact that Marsh had said he was an old man:

> Brother Thomas considers himself very aged and infirm, and you can see that he is, brethren and sisters. What is the cause of it? He left the Gospel of salvation. What do you think the difference is between his age and mine? One year and seven months to a day; and he is one year, seven months, and fourteen days older than Brother Heber C. Kimball.
>
> "Mormonism" keeps men and women young and handsome; and when they are full of the Spirit of God, there are none of them but what will have a glow upon their countenances; and that is what makes you and me young; for the Spirit of God is with us and within us.[8]

"David . . . I command you to bear record of what you now see and hear"

In an attempt to discredit the Book of Mormon, some contended that Joseph hypnotized the three witnesses, Oliver Cowdery, Martin Harris, and David Whitmer. "One critic wrote: 'At an early age he had what only the most gifted revivalist preachers could boast of—the talent for making men see visions.'"[9]

Joseph gave the following account of the sacred experience in a grove of trees close to the Whitmer home:

> We . . . had not been many minutes engaged in prayer, when presently we beheld a light above us in the air, of exceeding brightness; and behold, an angel stood before us. In his hands he held the plates which we had been praying for these to have a view of. He turned over the leaves one by one, so that we could see them, and discern the engravings thereon distinctly.
>
> He then addressed himself to David Whitmer, and said, "David, blessed is the Lord, and he that keeps His commandments;" when, immediately afterwards, we heard a voice from out of the bright light above us, saying, "These plates have been revealed by the power of God, and they have been translated by the power of God. The translation

of them which you have seen is correct, and I command you to bear record of what you now see and hear."[10]

The sacred events of that beautiful day radically changed the lives of the three men who became the special witnesses of the Book of Mormon. Later in life all three became discouraged with the Prophet and the practices of the Church, but they always asserted their testimonies. It would have been so easy for a hypnotized or an unconvinced person to deny his testimony. At times rewards and monies were offered if they would deny what they had claimed.

The degree of their conviction and their obedience to the commands of the Lord are shown in the following statement David Whitmer published more than half a century later to refute a charge that he had denied his testimony:

> It [was] represented by one John Murphy, of Polo, Caldwell County, Mo., that I, in a conversation with him last summer, denied my testimony as one of the three witnesses to the "Book of Mormon."
>
> To the end, therefore, that he may understand me now, if he did not then; and that the world may know the truth, I wish now, standing as it were, in the very sunset of life, and in the fear of God, once for all to make this public statement:
>
> That I have never at any time denied that testimony or any part thereof, which has so long since been published with that Book, as one of the three witnesses. Those who know me best, well know that I have always adhered to that testimony. And that no man may be misled or doubt my present views in regard to the same, I do again affirm the truth of all my statements, as then made and published.
>
> "He that hath an ear to hear, let him hear;" it was no delusion! What is written is written, and he that readeth let him understand.[11]

Yes, all three stood firm, obeyed the voice of God, and never denied what they had seen or experienced. Their testimonies shall forever serve as a testimony that Joseph Smith was indeed a prophet of God.

Why did some of the brethren desert the cause?

The Lord, through his young prophet, Joseph, promised the Saints great blessings if they would survive their trials:

> For verily I say unto you, blessed is he that keepeth my commandments, whether in life or in death; and he that is faithful in tribulation, the reward of the same is greater in the kingdom of heaven.
>
> Ye cannot behold with your natural eyes, for the present time, the design of your God concerning those things which shall come hereafter, and the glory which shall follow after much tribulation.
>
> For after much tribulation comes the blessings. Wherefore the day cometh that ye shall be crowned with much glory; the hour is not yet, but is nigh at hand. (D&C 58:2–4.)

Often Joseph expressed his concern to his brethren about obedience, with kind phrases:

> This is the word of the Lord to us, and we must, yea, the Lord helping us, we will obey: as on conditions of our obedience He has promised us great things; yea, even a visit from the heavens to honor us with His own presence. We greatly fear before the Lord lest we should fail of this great honor, which our Master proposes to confer on us; we are seeking for humility and great faith lest we be ashamed in His presence.[12]

> Therefore let your heart be comforted; live in strict obedience to the commandments of God, and walk humbly before Him, and He will exalt thee in His own due time.[13]

However, several of the brethren failed to respond properly and fell by the wayside. Some just became inactive, others became apostates and fought against their former friends. Why did this happen?

Few people now living can appreciate the pressure put upon the early brethren to deny their testimonies and desert their Prophet. Joseph, like Christ, was easy to love and follow, but in the heat of the battle, because of the threats on their lives and the persecution of their families, some of his dearest friends denied him. A good example was the fall and winter of 1838 in Missouri, after the mob militia had subjugated Far West: "A few days after his arrival Gen. Clark. . . . assembled the multitude on the temple square and delivered to them a written speech. . . . It goes far to prove that General Clark was ordered to 'exterminate' the Mormons, not excepting the women and children, and burn their houses and otherwise destroy their property."[14]

Following is part of General Clark's harangue to the brethren.

Gentlemen, you whose names are not attached to this list of names, will now have the privilege of going to your fields and providing corn, wood, etc., for your families. Those who are now taken will go from this to prison, be tried, and receive the due demerit of their crimes. . . .

. . . The character of this state has suffered almost beyond redemption, from the character, conduct and influence that you have exerted, and we deem it an act of justice to restore her character to its former standing among the states, by every proper means.

The orders of the governor to me were, that you should be exterminated, and not allowed to remain in the state, and had your leaders not been given up, and the terms of the treaty complied with, before this, you and your families would have been destroyed and your houses in ashes.

There is a discretionary power vested in my hands which I shall exercise in your favor for a season; for this lenity you are indebted to my clemency. I do not say that you shall go now, but you must not think of staying here another season, or of putting in crops, for the moment you do this the citizens will be upon you. If I am called here again, in case of a non-compliance of a treaty made, do not think that I shall act any more as I have done—you need not expect any mercy, but extermination, for I am determined the governor's order shall be executed. As for your leaders, do not once think—do not imagine for a moment—do not let it enter your mind that they will be delivered, or that you will see their faces again, for their fate is fixed—their die is cast—their doom is sealed.

I am sorry, gentlemen, to see so great a number of apparently intelligent men found in the situation that you are; and oh! that I could invoke that *Great Spirit, the unknown God,* to rest upon you, and make you sufficiently intelligent to break that chain of superstition, and liberate you from those fetters of fanaticism with which you are bound—that you no longer worship a man.

I would advise you to scatter abroad, and never again organize yourselves with Bishops, Presidents, etc., lest you excite the jealousies of the people, and subject yourselves to the same calamities that have now come upon you.

You have always been the aggressors—you have brought upon yourselves these difficulties by being disaffected and not being subject to rule—and my advice is, that you become as other citizens, lest by a recurrence of these events you bring upon yourselves irretrievable ruin.[15]

Several days prior to this,

the mob (called Governor's troops) . . . marched into town, and under pretense of searching for arms, tore up floors, upset haystacks, plundered the most valuable effects they could lay their hands on, wantonly wasted and destroyed a great amount of property, compelled the brethren at the point of the bayonet to sign deeds of trust to pay the expenses of the mob, even while the place was desecrated by the chastity of women being violated. About eighty men were taken prisoners, the remainder were ordered to leave the state, and were forbidden, under threat of being shot by the mob to assemble more than three in a place. . . .

Myself [Joseph Smith] and fellow prisoners were taken to the town, into the public square, and before our departure we, after much entreaty, were suffered to see our families, being attended all the while by a strong guard. I found my wife and children in tears, who feared we had been shot by those who had sworn to take our lives, and that they would see me no more. When I entered my house, they clung to my garments, their eyes streaming with tears, while mingled emotions of joy and sorrow were manifested in their countenances. I requested to have a private interview with them a few minutes, but this privilege was denied me by the guard. I was then obliged to take my departure.

Who can realize the feelings which I experienced at that

time, to be thus torn from my companion, and leave her
surrounded with monsters in the shape of men, and my
children, too, not knowing how their wants would be sup-
plied; while I was to be taken far from them in order that
my enemies might destroy me when they thought proper to
do so. My partner wept, my children clung to me, until they
were thrust from me by the swords of the guards. I felt
overwhelmed while I witnessed the scene, and could only
recommend them to the care of that God whose kindness
had followed me to the present time, and who alone could
protect them, and deliver me from the hands of my enemies, and restore me to my family.[16]

13

Physical Appearance
and Strength

Here, then, is eternal life—to know the only wise and true God: and you have got to learn how to be Gods yourselves . . . the same as all Gods have done before you, namely, by going from one small degree to another, and from a small capacity to a great one; from grace to grace, from exaltation to exaltation, until you . . . are able to . . . sit in glory, as do those who sit enthroned in everlasting power![1]

—Joseph Smith

A fine looking man

In his day, Joseph Smith was an exceptionally large man, although slightly smaller in stature than his brother Hyrum. Joseph was about six feet one inch tall and weighed over two hundred pounds, very little if any of which was fat. He had piercing blue eyes that seemed to read the hearts of men. George Q. Cannon said: "His head, crowned with a mass of soft, wavy [brown] hair, was grandly poised. . . . He wore no beard, and the full strength and beauty of his countenance impressed all beholders at a glance. . . . His physical person was the fit habitation of his exalted spirit. . . . His face possessed a complexion of such clearness and transparency that the soul appeared to shine through."[2]

Josiah Quincy said, "A fine looking man is what the passerby would instinctively have murmured upon meeting the remarkable individual."[3]

A Mr. Davis, writing to his wife, said that Joseph was "what you ladies would call a very good looking man."[4]

Josiah Quincy added that of all men he had met, Joseph Smith was one of two who "seemed best endowed with that kingly faculty which directs, as by intrinsic right, the feeble or confused souls who are looking for guidance."[5]

Parley P. Pratt said, "There was something connected with the serene and steady penetrating glance of his eye, as if he would penetrate the deepest abyss of the human heart, gaze into eternity, penetrate the heavens, and comprehend all worlds."[6]

Brigham Young said, "I feel like shouting hallelujah, all the time, when I think that I ever knew Joseph Smith, the Prophet."[7]

He boasted that he could easily throw Joseph Smith

Joseph was vigorous physically. He enjoyed contests of wrestling, but it was more than wrestling—it was a free-for-all. Joseph had the reputation of being an outstanding wrestler. He was lithe and lean, big and strong, and, having lived in the frontier environment, was used to the competitiveness of the day.

Many years after the Prophet's imprisonment there Andrew Jenson visited Liberty Jail. In the town he met "James H. Ford, an ex-official, 72 years old, who served as deputy sheriff of Clay County in 1838–39, and had Joseph Smith and fellow-prisoners under his charge during their incarceration." Andrew Jenson recorded as follows an incident Ford related to him.

> Mr. Ford also accompanied the prisoners to Gallatin, Daviess County, in April, 1839, and said when they arrived there, they were handed over to some half-a-dozen of the strongest and roughest men of Daviess County, who at first crowded the prisoners into a corner of a room, refusing to allow them any liberties at all, but after a little, when they began to converse with the prisoners, they became quite sociable with them, and a reputed champion wrestler of Daviess County wanted to try strength with the "Mormon" Prophet. Joseph excused himself saying, he was a prisoner and could not engage in exercises of that kind under the circumstances; but finally, through the solicitations of the guard and the man promising not to get angry if he was thrown, Joseph consented to wrestle with him. Consequently a ring was made and the two stepped forth.

The Missourian took recourse to all the trickery known to him in the art of wrestling, but was unsuccessful in his attempts to throw Joseph. Finally the latter gathered up his strength, made a first real attempt and threw his opponent flat upon his back in a pool of water. This made the fellow mad, although he had agreed not to get offended if thrown, and he wished to fight, but the guard interfered and the Daviess County champion was much humiliated afterwards in being made the object of considerable ridicule on the part of his companions, he having previously boasted that he could easily throw Joseph Smith.[8]

Strangers coming from a distance to see the Prophet knew him on sight

Many accounts reveal that strangers coming from a distance to see the Prophet knew him on sight. Jane James, one of several black converts to join the Church during its early years, walked with her family one thousand miles from Connecticut to see him and to make their home with the Saints. She recalled recognizing him when she first saw him as she had seen him in a vision before she left her native state.[9]

George Q. Cannon, fifteen years of age, arriving at the Nauvoo wharf with his father from England (his mother having died and been buried at sea), while still on the docked steamer pointed out the Prophet to his father and declared he would have "known him among ten thousand."[10]

Emmeline B. Wells, a convert from Massachusetts, recognized the Prophet in a large crowd. When he shook her hand she was "simply electrified," thrilled through and through every part of her body. She was to say of the experience, "The one thought that filled my soul was, I have seen the Prophet of God, he has taken me by the hand, and this testimony has never left me in all the 'perils by the way.' "[11]

Joseph, the Prophet, affected thousands of people that way, members and nonmembers alike. One such experience happened to Dan Jones, a short, sturdy Welshman who had settled in Augusta, about ten miles north of Nauvoo. Here he and Levi Moffitt built and operated a small steamboat which they named the *Maid of Iowa*. Some of the English converts traveled up the Mississippi to Nauvoo on this steamboat.

One day as his steamer landed at the Nauvoo dock with a load of English converts, the Prophet Joseph stepped on board, went up to Dan, and said, "God bless this little man." Dan Jones was touched by the Prophet's kindness and blessing. He was baptized in Nauvoo the same year.[12] Dan Jones became a great friend to the Prophet and served a most successful mission to his native Wales.

"His physical person was the fit habitation of his exalted spirit"

George Q. Cannon wrote a powerful description of Joseph Smith.

Joseph Smith had been a retiring youth—the Spirit made him bold to declare to rulers and potentates and all mankind, the gospel again revealed. He had been a humble farmer lad—divine authority sat so becomingly upon him that men looked at him with reverent awe. He had been unlearned in the great things of art and science—he walked with God until human knowledge was to his eye an open book, the celestial light beamed through his mind.

His lofty soul comprehended the grandeur of his mission upon earth; and with divine fortitude he fulfilled the destiny which God had ordained for him before the world was.

. . . His physical person was the fit habitation of his exalted spirit. He was more than six feet in height, with expansive chest and clean-cut limbs—a staunch and graceful figure. His head, crowned with a mass of soft, wavy hair, was grandly poised. His face possessed a complexion of such clearness and transparency that the soul appeared to shine through. He wore no beard, and the full strength and beauty of his countenance impressed all beholders at a glance. He had eyes which seemed to read the hearts of men. His mouth was one of mingled power and sweetness. His majesty of air was natural, not studied. Though full of personal and prophetic dignity whenever occasion demanded, he could at other times unbend and be as happy and unconventional as a boy. . . .

But whether engaging in manly sport, during hours of

relaxation, or proclaiming words of wisdom in pulpit or grove, he was ever the leader. His magnetism was masterful, and his heroic qualities won universal admiration. Where he moved all classes were forced to recognize in him the man of power. Strangers journeying to see him from a distance, knew him the moment their eyes beheld his person. Men have crossed ocean and continent to meet him, and have selected him instantly from among a multitude.[13]

"Reared in the backwoods of New York— never looked inside a college or high school"

For his book *Joseph Smith, an American Prophet,* which was published in 1933 (when the Church had less than a million members) John Henry Evans penned these impressive words about the Prophet:

> Here is a man who was born in the stark hills of Vermont; who was reared in the backwoods of New York; who never looked inside a college or high school; who lived in six States, no one of which would own him during his lifetime; who spent months in the vile prisons of the period; who, even when he had his freedom, was hounded like a fugitive; who was covered once with a coat of tar and feathers, and left for dead; who, with his following, was driven by irate neighbors from New York to Ohio, from Ohio to Missouri, and Missouri to Illinois; and who, at the unripe age of thirty-eight, was shot to death by a mob with painted faces.
>
> Yet this man became mayor of the biggest town in Illinois and the state's most prominent citizen, the commander of the largest body of trained soldiers in the nation outside the Federal army, the founder of cities and of a university, and aspired to become President of the United States.
>
> He wrote a book which has baffled the literary critics for a hundred years and which is today more widely read than any other volume save the Bible. On the threshold of an organizing age he established the most nearly perfect social mechanism in the modern world, and developed a religious philosophy that challenges anything of the kind in history,

for completeness and cohesion. And he set up the machinery for an economic system that would take the brood of Fears out of the heart of man—the fear of want through sickness, old age, unemployment, and poverty.

In thirty nations are men and women who look upon him as a greater leader than Moses and a greater prophet than Isaiah; his disciples now number close to a million and already a granite shaft pierces the sky over the place where he was born, and another over the place where he is credited with having received the inspiration for his Book.[14]

14

Prayer

The best way to obtain truth and wisdom is not to ask it from books, but to go to God in prayer, and obtain divine teaching. . . . There is never a time when the spirit is too old to approach God![1]

—Joseph Smith

"If any of you lack wisdom, let him ask of God"

When the Prophet's brother William was asked, "What caused Joseph to ask for guidance as to what church he ought to join?" he replied:

> Why, there was a joint revival . . . in the neighborhood between the Baptists, Methodists, and Presbyterians, and they had succeeded in stirring up quite a feeling and after the meeting the question arose which church should have the converts?
>
> Rev. Stockton was the president of the meeting and suggested that it was their meeting and under their care, and they had a church there and they ought to join the Presbyterians, but as father did not like Rev. Stockton very well, our folks hesitated and the next evening a Rev. Mr. Lane of the Methodists preached a sermon on "what church shall I join," and the burden of his discourses was to ask God, using as a text "If any man lack wisdom let him ask of God, who giveth to all men liberally." And of course when Joseph went home and was looking over the text, he was impressed to do just what the preacher had said.[2]

The First Vision

Joseph Smith's own history records the events leading up to and including the First Vision.

>   I was at this time in my fifteenth year. My father's family was proselyted to the Presbyterian faith, and four of them joined that church, namely, my mother, Lucy; my brothers Hyrum and Samuel Harrison; and my sister Sophronia.
>   During this time of great excitement my mind was called up to serious reflection and great uneasiness; but though my feelings were deep and often poignant, still I kept myself aloof from all these parties, though I attended their several meetings as often as occasion would permit. In process of time my mind became somewhat partial to the Methodist sect, and I felt some desire to be united with them; but so great were the confusion and strife among the different denominations, that it was impossible for a person young as I was, and so unacquainted with men and things, to come to any certain conclusion who was right and who was wrong.
>   My mind at times was greatly excited, the cry and tumult were so great and incessant. The Presbyterians were most decided against the Baptists and Methodists, and used all the powers of both reason and sophistry to prove their errors, or, at least, to make the people think they were in error. On the other hand, the Baptists and Methodists in their turn were equally zealous in endeavoring to establish their own tenets and disprove all others.
>   In the midst of this war of words and tumult of opinions, I often said to myself: What is to be done? Who of all these parties are right; or, are they all wrong together? If any one of them be right, which is it, and how shall I know it?
>   While I was laboring under the extreme difficulties caused by the contests of these parties of religionists, I was one day reading the Epistle of James, first chapter and fifth verse, which reads: *If any of you lack wisdom, let him ask of God, that giveth to all men liberally, and upbraideth not; and it shall be given him.*
>   Never did any passage of scripture come with more power

to the heart of man that this did at this time to mine. It seemed to enter with great force into every feeling of my heart. I reflected on it again and again, knowing that if any person needed wisdom from God, I did; for how to act I did not know, and unless I could get more wisdom than I then had, I would never know; for the teachers of religion of the different sects understood the same passages of scripture so differently as to destroy all confidence in settling the question by an appeal to the Bible.

At length I came to the conclusion that I must either remain in darkness and confusion, or else I must do as James directs, that is, ask of God. I at length came to the determination to "ask of God," concluding that if he gave wisdom to them that lacked wisdom, and would give liberally, and not upbraid, I might venture.

So, in accordance with this, my determination to ask of God, I retired to the woods to make the attempt. It was on the morning of a beautiful, clear day, early in the spring of eighteen hundred and twenty. It was the first time in my life that I had made such an attempt, for amidst all my anxieties I had never as yet made the attempt to pray vocally.

After I had retired to the place where I had previously designed to go, having looked around me, and finding myself alone, I kneeled down and began to offer up the desires of my heart to God. I had scarcely done so, when immediately I was seized upon by some power which entirely overcame me, and had such an astonishing influence over me as to bind my tongue so that I could not speak. Thick darkness gathered around me, and it seemed to me for a time as if I were doomed to sudden destruction.

But, exerting all my powers to call upon God to deliver me out of the power of this enemy which had seized upon me, and at the very moment when I was ready to sink into despair and abandon myself to destruction—not to an imaginary ruin, but to the power of some actual being from the unseen world, who had such marvelous power as I had never before felt in any being—just at this moment of great alarm, I saw a pillar of light exactly over my head, above the brightness of the sun, which descended gradually until it fell upon me.

It no sooner appeared than I found myself delivered from the enemy which held me bound. When the light rested upon me I saw two Personages, whose brightness and glory defy all description, standing above me in the air. One of them spake unto me, calling me by name and said, pointing to the other—*This is My Beloved Son. Hear Him!*

My object in going to inquire of the Lord was to know which of all the sects was right, that I might know which to join. No sooner, therefore, did I get possession of myself, so as to be able to speak, than I asked the Personages who stood above me in the light, which of all the sects was right (for at this time it had never entered into my heart that all were wrong)—and which I should join.

I was answered that I must join none of them, for they were all wrong; and the Personage who addressed me said that all their creeds were an abomination in his sight; that those professors were all corrupt; that: "they draw near to me with their lips, but their hearts are far from me, they teach for doctrines the commandments of men, having a form of godliness, but they deny the power thereof."

He again forbade me to join with any of them; and many other things did he say unto me, which I cannot write at this time. When I came to myself again, I found myself lying on my back, looking up into heaven. When the light had departed, I had no strength; but soon recovering in some degree, I went home. And as I leaned up to the fireplace, mother inquired what the matter was. I replied, "Never mind, all is well—I am well enough off." I then said to my mother, "I have learned for myself that Presbyterianism is not true." (Joseph Smith—History 1:7–20.)

"We passed on without interruption"

As recorded in *History of the Church*, Joseph and others, because of mighty prayer, went past their enemies and were not recognized.

Towards the latter end of August, in company with John and David Whitmer, and my brother Hyrum Smith, I visited the Church at Colesville, New York. Well knowing the determined hostility of our enemies in that quarter, and also knowing that it was our duty to visit the Church, we had called upon our Heavenly Father, in mighty prayer, that He would grant us an opportunity of meeting with them, that he would blind the eyes of our enemies, so that they would not know us, and that we might on this occasion return unmolested.

Our prayers were not in vain, for when within a little distance of Mr. Knight's place, we encountered a large company at work upon the public road, amongst whom were several of our most bitter enemies. They looked earnestly at us, but not knowing us, we passed on without interruption. That evening we assembled the Church, and confirmed them, partook of the Sacrament, and held a happy meeting, having much reason to rejoice in the God of our salvation, and sing hosannas to His holy name.

Next morning we set out on our return home, and although our enemies had offered a reward of five dollars to any one who would give them information of our arrival, yet did we get out of the neighborhood, without the least annoyance, and arrived home in safety. Some few days afterwards, however, Newel Knight came to my place, and from him we learned that, very shortly after our departure, the mob came to know of our having been there, when they immediately collected together, and threatened the brethren, and very much annoyed them during all that day.[3]

"I knew the Lord would answer my prayer"

[Joseph Smith] sat down to eat a scanty meal of corn bread, and prayed, "Lord, we thank Thee for this johnny cake, and ask Thee to send us something better. Amen." Before the bread had been eaten, a man came to the door and asked if Joseph were home, and upon being informed that he was, said, "I have brought you some flour and a ham." After thanking the man and blessing him for the gift, the Prophet turned to his wife and said, "I knew the Lord would answer my prayer."[4]

"I saw mother kneeling . . . asking God, in tears, to spare our lives"

When Zion's Camp was stricken with cholera, several of the brethren died. Joseph and Hyrum were commanded not to try to heal them, because this was the will of God. They, too, were stricken with a very severe cramp, and some thought even the Prophet might perish. Three times Joseph and Hyrum knelt to beg the Lord for his healing influence. They later told the story to their mother.

> "We then kneeled down the third time, concluding never to rise to our feet again until one or the other should get a testimony that we should be healed; and that the one who should get the first intimation of the same from the Spirit, should make it known to the other."
>
> . . . After praying some time the cramp began to release its hold, and, in a short time, Hyrum sprang to his feet and exclaimed, "Joseph, we shall return to our families. I have had an open vision, in which I saw mother kneeling under an apple tree; and she is even now asking God, in tears, to spare our lives, that she may again behold us in the flesh. The Spirit testifies, that her prayers, united with ours, will be answered."
>
> "Oh, my mother!" said Joseph, "how often have your prayers been the means of assisting us when the shadows of death encompassed us."[5]

The Lord had heard the boy's prayer

Joseph taught that parents must "teach their children to pray, and to walk uprightly before the Lord" (D&C 68:28). For "little" children are alive in Christ" (Moroni 8:12).

> One evening as he was walking with his bodyguards (and with the threats upon his life, he needed them) Joseph passed a door that was slightly ajar. Inside was a little boy kneeling in prayer, asking that Joseph would be safe from his enemies.
>
> The Prophet turned to the guards and said that they might all go to bed and sleep soundly, for the Lord had heard the boy's prayer, and no harm would befall them that night.[6]

"You've prayed me here, now what do you want of me?"

Jesus taught that "whatsoever ye shall ask the Father in my name, which is right, believing that ye shall receive, behold it shall be given unto you" (3 Nephi 18:20). But few prayers are answered by a direct visitation from heavenly visitors; most are answered by other people inspired by the Holy Ghost to do things which meet the needs of those who are praying. A good example of this happened to Elizabeth Ann and Newel Whitney.

The Whitneys were a religious people who studied the Bible and prayed sincerely to their Heavenly Father. They had been Campbellites, until they were baptized when Parley P. Pratt and Oliver Cowdery brought the gospel to them while proselyting the Kirtland area on their way to their mission to the Lamanites. "Mother Whitney," as she was known, told the story: One night, in February 1831, "while she and her husband were praying to the Lord to know how they might obtain the gift of the Holy Ghost, which of all things they desired, they saw a vision as of a cloud of glory resting upon their house, and heard a voice from heaven saying, 'Prepare to receive the word of the Lord, for it is coming.'"

> About the first of February, 1831, a sleigh containing four persons drove through the streets of Kirtland and drew up in front of the store of Gilbert and Whitney. One of the men, a young and stalwart personage alighted, and springing up the steps walked into the store and to where [Newel Whitney] the junior partner [who had recently joined the Church] was standing. 'Newel K. Whitney! Thou art the man!' he exclaimed, extending his hand cordially, as if to an old and familiar acquaintance.
>
> "You have the advantage of me," replied the merchant, as he mechanically took the proffered hand, "I could not call you by name as you have me."
>
> "I am Joseph the Prophet," said the stranger smiling. "You've prayed me here, now what do you want of me?"[7]

The Prophet Joseph, while still in New York, had seen the Whitneys, in a dream, praying for his coming to Kirtland, Ohio. Joseph and Emma later lived in the home of the Whitneys, who gave freely of their means to support the couple's needs.

"Joseph Smith in Front of the Kirtland Temple," by Robert T. Barrett.
Used by permission of the artist.

15

Service

If thou lovest me thou shalt serve me and keep all my commandments.

—D&C 42:29

I tell you these things that ye may learn wisdom; that ye may learn that when ye are in the service of your fellow beings ye are only in the service of your God.

—Mosiah 2:17

"I love to wait upon the Saints"

As Nauvoo began to grow, Joseph opened a store to help provide food, clothing, and tools to the Saints. The gospel which he preached was one of temporal salvation and happiness as well as spiritual exaltation. He was always willing to do his share of the work with a smile. In opening the store, he said:

"I rejoice that we have been enabled to do as well as we have, for the hearts of many of the poor brethren and sisters will be made glad with these comforts which are now within their reach."

In a letter to Brother Edward Hunter, under date of January 5, 1842, the Prophet shows his humility and the love of his heart in these words:

"The store has been filled to overflowing and I have stood behind the counter all day, distributing goods as steadily as any clerk you ever saw, to oblige those who were compelled to go without their Christmas and New Year's dinners for the want of a little sugar, molasses, raisins, etc.; and to please myself also, for I love to wait upon the Saints and to be a servant to all, hoping that I may be exalted in the due time of the Lord."[1]

"You should receive a witness that your faith may be strengthened"

Living in Harmony, Pennsylvania, was a very difficult time for the young Prophet and his wife, Emma. They lost their first son at birth, and almost lost Emma. Then Martin Harris lost the first 116 pages of Book of Mormon manuscript. The angel Moroni took the plates and the Urim and Thummim from Joseph, and it was some while before he returned them. And as prejudice against Joseph grew in the neighborhood, Emma's father turned against him and exhibited bitter feelings toward him.

As persecution increased, Oliver wrote to his friend David Whitmer about their problems. David and his parents invited Oliver, Joseph, and Emma to come and live with them in Fayette, New York. While David was on his way, Joseph saw him in vision coming to get them in a wagon, and David was astonished at their readiness to leave when he arrived.

While they were living in the Whitmer home, an event occurred that we may consider a foretaste of a promise the Lord has made: "I the Lord . . . delight to honor those who serve me in righteousness and truth unto the end. . . . And to them will I reveal all . . . mysteries of my kingdom. . . . Yea, even the wonders of eternity shall they know, and things to come I will show them." (D&C 76:5, 7–8.)

David Whitmer reported as follows:

> Some time after [Joseph, Emma, and Oliver's arrival], my mother was going to milk the cows when she was met out near the yard by the same old man [who had carried the plates there] . . . who said to her: "You have been very faithful and diligent in your labors, but you are tired because of the increase of your toil; it is proper therefore that you should receive a witness that your faith may be strengthened." Thereupon he showed her the plates.
>
> My father and mother had a large family of their own, the addition to it therefore of Joseph, his wife Emma and

Oliver very greatly increased the toil and anxiety of my mother. And although she had never complained she had sometimes felt that her labor was too much, or at least she was perhaps beginning to feel so. This circumstance, however, completely removed all such feelings and nerved her up for her increased responsibilities.[2]

"The angel said that the Lord would send me a scribe, and I trust his promise to be verified"

Many have asked the question, why would a young school teacher, Oliver Cowdery, leave his profession so quickly to become the full-time scribe of Joseph Smith? While the rest of the world around him laughed and made fun of Joseph, or persecuted him to try and see his "Golden Bible," Oliver, after seeing Joseph for less than two days, dropped everything else to become his faithful unpaid scribe.

Joseph badly needed a scribe. After losing their first child at birth his wife, Emma, wasn't well enough to serve as his scribe; Martin Harris had proven himself untrustworthy when he lost the first 116 pages of translated manuscript; and Joseph could not translate alone. Emma later told her son:

> The larger part of this labor [translation] was done in my presence and where I could see and know what was being done. . . . During no part of it did Joseph Smith have any manuscript or book of any kind from which to read or dictate except the metallic plates which I knew he had. . . . Joseph Smith could neither write nor dictate a coherent and well-worded letter, let alone dictate a book like the Book of Mormon. . . .
>
> The Book of Mormon is of divine authenticity—I have not the slightest doubt of it. . . . When acting as his scribe, [he] would dictate to me hour after hour; and when returning after meals, or after interruptions, he would at once begin where he had left off, without either seeing the manuscript or having any portion of it read to him. . . . It would have been improbable that a learned man could do this; and, for one so ignorant and unlearned as he was, it was simply impossible.[3]

But Joseph, as always, was optimistic. He told his family: "The angel said that the Lord would send me a scribe, and I trust his promise to be verified. The angel seemed pleased with me when he gave me back the Urim and Thummim, and he told me that the Lord loved me, for my faithfulness and humility."[4]

The Lord was true to his promise:

> On the 5th day of April, 1829, Oliver Cowdery came to my house, until which time I had never seen him. He stated to me that having been teaching school in the neighborhood where my father resided, and my father being one of those who sent [children] to the school, he went to board for a season at his house, and while there the family related to him the circumstance of my having received the plates, and accordingly he had come to make inquiries of me.
>
> Two days after the arrival of Mr. Cowdery (being the 7th of April) I commenced to translate the Book of Mormon, and he began to write for me . . . I inquired of the Lord through the Urim and Thummim, and obtained the following [revelation]. . . . :
>
> 21. Behold, I am Jesus Christ, the Son of God. I am the same that came unto mine own, and mine own received me not. I am the light which shineth in darkness, and the darkness comprehendeth it not.
>
> 22. Verily, verily, I say unto you, if you desire a further witness, cast your mind upon the night that you cried unto me in your heart, that you might know concerning the truth of these things.
>
> 23. Did I not speak peace to your mind concerning the matter? What greater witness can you have than from God?
>
> 24. And now, behold, you have received a witness; for if I have told you things which no man knoweth, have you not received a witness? [D&C 6:21–24]. . . .
>
> After we had received this revelation, Oliver Cowdery stated to me that after he had gone to my father's to board, and after the family had communicated to him concerning my having obtained the plates, that one night after he had retired to bed he called upon the Lord to know if these things were so, and the Lord manifested to him that they were true, but he had kept the circumstance entirely secret, and had mentioned it to no one; so that after this revelation was given, he knew that the work was true, because

no being living knew of the thing alluded to in the revelation, but God and himself.[5]

Finally the Book of Mormon is published: a new witness for Christ

Few people appreciate the sacrifice and service required by many to accomplish the great task of publishing the handwritten manuscript of the Book of Mormon as a hardbound book. Presses of the day, especially those in small towns like Palmyra, were designed to print single sheets of paper or simple two- or three-page documents. Even in the larger cities like Rochester a large run for a hardbound book was 1,000 copies.

Joseph, through prayer and guidance of the Spirit, felt that they should print 5,000 copies. This was a mammoth order, requiring nearly 400,000 eight-page signatures, which had to be cut, trimmed, and folded into 5,000 copies of a 590-page book. A printing company in Rochester, New York, was contacted but refused, presumably not wanting to take the financial risk and seeing no guarantor on the horizon.

Joseph considered taking his order to New York City or perhaps Philadelphia. While visiting his family in Palmyra, he approached Egbert B. Grandin, a young printer, of the local newspaper the *Wayne Sentinel.* He agreed to print the book for three thousand dollars. Joseph had never seen that much money in his whole life. In the 1820s a farm could be bought for that kind of money. Joseph was accustomed to work for fifty cents to a dollar a day. Where would he go for that kind of financial support?

Joseph turned for money to the man who had given him money before: Martin Harris. Even though Martin had lost the 116 pages of the manuscript and the Lord had called him a "wicked man" (D&C 3:12), he agreed to secure the contract with a mortgage and bond note on his farm, the debt to be paid in eighteen months. The note was signed in August, 1829.

To assure that nothing would be lost, Oliver made a handwritten copy of the manuscript, the printer's copy. Joseph was living in Harmony. Hyrum Smith or Oliver Cowdery took only a few pages of the printer's copy to the press at a time. Since it had very little punctuation or capitalization, John H. Gilbert, the typesetter at Grandin's press, was allowed to punctuate the book. The printing of the book proceeded despite hostile local efforts to stop the process.[6]

Several months into the printing, Palmyra and the surrounding areas were alive with talk about the soon-to-be-published "Gold Bible." A mass meeting was held and a resolution was passed by the townspeople pledging themselves not to purchase the Book of Mormon when it was published, and to use their influence to prevent others from purchasing it. This frightened Mr. Grandin, who held up printing until Joseph and Martin reassured him that he would be paid regardless of book sales.[7]

Finally the long-awaited day arrived. On March 26, 1830, the Book of Mormon went on sale at the Palmyra Book Store. The reception was cold. However, the believers rejoiced. The Church was organized a few days later on April 6, and optimism ran high. Samuel Smith was sent out as a missionary to sell the book;[8] however, sales did not materialize quickly, and Martin Harris was obliged to sell his farm to pay the debt to the printer. Eventually, however, he was repaid in full.[9]

The Lord confirmed his pleasure with the book when he said: "As your Lord and your God liveth it is true" (D&C 17:6).

Then he added this wonderful promise: "And those who receive it in faith, and work righteousness, shall receive a crown of eternal life; but those who harden their hearts in unbelief, and reject it, it shall turn to their own condemnation" (D&C 20:14–15).

"I have no desire but to do all men good"

Joseph loved to serve people, but he was kind and gentle in his approach. The following 1843 comment shows his love for others and his willingness to sacrifice his own life for the cause:

> I know what I say; I understand my mission and business. God Almighty is my shield; and what can man do if God is my friend? I shall not be sacrificed until my time comes; then I shall be offered freely. All flesh is as grass, and a governor is no better than other men; when he dies he is but a bag of dust.

I thank God for preserving me from my enemies; I have no enemies but for the truth's sake. I have no desire but to do all men good. I feel to pray for all men. We don't ask any people to throw away any good they have got; we only ask them to come and get more.

What if all the world should embrace this Gospel? They would then see eye to eye, and the blessings of God would be poured out upon the people, which is the desire of my whole soul.[10]

"Joseph Smith in Liberty Jail," by Greg K. Olsen.
Courtesy of Jack and Marie Lake.

16

Stress

*Be not weary in well-doing, for ye are laying the founda-
tion of a great work. And out of small things proceedeth
that which is great.*

—D&C 64:33

"When I am with the boys I make all
the fun I can for them"

When Porter Rockwell was in jail, in Missouri, his
mother went to see him at the jail, and the Missourians told
her that if she would raise a certain amount of money and
give it to them they would let her son go. Joseph started out
to get the money. He came to a large crowd of young men
who were wrestling, that being the popular sport in those
days. Among the boys there was a bully, from LaHarpe I believe. He had thrown down every one on the ground who
wrestled with him. When Joseph came to the crowd he told
them what he wanted, passed around the hat, raised what
money he could and then went into the ring to take part
with the young men and boys in their games. So he was invited to wrestle with this bully.

The man was eager to have a tussle with the Prophet, so
Joseph stepped forward and took hold of the man. The first
pass he made, Joseph whirled him around and took him by
the collar and seat of his trousers and walked out to a ditch
and threw him in it. Then, taking him by the arm, he
helped him up and patted him on the back and said, "You
must not mind this. When I am with the boys I make all the
fun I can for them."[1]

"It was just so with his mind; he did not want it strung up all the time"

Elder William M. Allred says he once heard the Prophet justify himself for playing with the young people by relating this story:

"A certain prophet . . . was sitting under the shade of a tree amusing himself in some way, when a hunter came along with his bow and arrow and reproved him. The prophet asked him if he kept his bow strung up all the time. The hunter answered that he did not. The prophet asked him why, and he said it would lose its elasticity if he did. The Prophet said it was just so with his mind; he did not want it strung up all the time."[2]

"All these things shall give thee experience, and shall be for thy good"

Few can appreciate the stress, the pain, and the suffering of Joseph Smith and his companions as they spent the four long months, including the Christmas season, in a cold, dreary dungeon—Liberty Jail. Imagine being confined from December 1, 1938, until April 6, 1839, in a small, cold jail measuring only twenty by twenty-two feet, with no heat, nor light, nor running water; confined to this place day and night. Meals were coarse, conditions filthy, visitors were few, and reports of murder, rape, and general hatred were constant as twelve thousand of the Prophet's followers were driven from their Missouri homes and farms in the cold of winter.

The fate of loved ones was unknown to Joseph, but their suffering was almost greater than could be borne. His beloved Emma was forced to live with friends and try to survive with their adopted daughter, Julia, and their three small sons, Joseph III, Frederick, and Alexander (who was only six months old). Yet at this time God chose to speak to his young prophet, giving him what is now contained in sections 121, 122, and 123 of the Doctrine and Covenants. Because of the Prophet's deep communion with God and the nature of the revelations given, B. H. Roberts, an early Church historian, called the

Liberty Jail the "prison-temple."[3] Under such trying circumstances the Lord told Joseph:

> My son, peace be unto thy soul; thine adversity and thine afflictions shall be but a small moment;
> And then, if thou endure it well, God shall exalt thee on high; thou shalt triumph over all thy foes.
> Thy friends do stand by thee, and they shall hail thee again with warm hearts and friendly hands. (D&C 121:7–9.)

> If the very jaws of hell shall gape open the mouth wide after thee, know thou, my son, that all these things shall give thee experience, and shall be for thy good.
> The Son of Man hath descended below them all. Art thou greater than he?
> . . . Fear not what man can do, for God shall be with you forever and ever. (D&C 122:7–9.)

> Therefore, dearly beloved brethren, let us cheerfully do all things that lie in our power (D&C 123:17).

Never be discouraged

[Joseph] thrived on opposition. All his life he swam upstream against a strong current full of eddies, underwashes, and rapids. At every stroke some obstruction sprang up to block his way. He experienced more than one defeat. But he was never disheartened to the point where he gave up. "Never be discouraged," the Prophet said once to his cousin, George A. Smith: "if I were sunk in the lowest pit of Nova Scotia, with the Rocky Mountains piled on me, I would hang on, exercise faith, and keep up good courage, and I would come out on top." This battling spirit in Joseph Smith, prophet though he claimed to be, never failed to leave its secret thrill in the heart of every American who knew of it.[4]

"There has seldom . . . been a happier people upon the earth than the Church of the Saints now were"

The Saints had been told in the summer of 1831 that Zion would be established in Missouri, and within two years "immigration had poured into [Jackson County]," where Church members "now numbered upwards of one thousand souls." There was a clash of cultures as these industrious pioneers settled among the backwoods frontier people of Missouri. Parley P. Pratt recorded:

[The Saints] had all purchased lands and paid for them, and most of them were improving in buildings. . . . and the wilderness became a fruitful field. . . .

They lived in peace and quiet; no lawsuits with each other or with the world; few or no debts were contracted; few promises broken; there were no thieves, robbers, or murderers; few or no idlers; all seemed to worship God with a ready heart. On Sundays the people assembled to preach, pray, sing, and receive the ordinances of God. Other days all seemed busy in the various pursuits of industry. In short, there has seldom, if ever, been a happier people upon the earth than the Church of the Saints now were![5]

The peace and quiet was short lived, for soon the success of the Saints created such a rift between them and the early residents of Missouri that literally thousands of Saints were driven from their homes in bitter winter. Although the outcome was not what the Saints had had in mind, from the above snapshot of time we can see a pattern of how to be a happy people.

"Let us keep cool as a cucumber on a frosty morning"

Controlling stress and remaining calm in a tense moment can be a great challenge. The Prophet did not retaliate when he was wronged or spoken to harshly or persecuted.

The Bible clearly teaches: "Recompense to no man evil for evil. . . . Live peaceably with all men. . . . Avenge not yourselves, but rather give place unto wrath: for it is written, Vengeance is mine; I will repay, saith the Lord. Therefore if thine enemy hunger, feed him; if he thirst, give him drink. . . . Be not overcome of evil, but overcome evil with good." (Romans 12:17–21.) The Lord reemphasized through Joseph, "If men will smite you, or your families . . . and ye bear it patiently and revile not against them, neither seek revenge, ye shall be rewarded" (D&C 98:23).

At a time of crisis in Nauvoo, Joseph gave the people exemplary counsel. The Prophet's enemies from Missouri had attempted to kidnap him, and false brethren were plotting against his life. He assigned forty policemen to patrol the city of Nauvoo to maintain law and order. At this time of great concern, gun salesmen came to Nauvoo to sell the Mormons revolving pistols. As mayor of Nauvoo Joseph addressed the new policemen:

> We will be at peace with all men, so long as they mind their own business and let us alone. Even "Peace with Missouri". . . if they will stop their persecution and oppressive warfare against us. . . .
>
> Let us keep cool as a cucumber on a frosty morning. Do not be excited. . . .
>
> Don't buy [the guns]: it would be better to buy ploughshares and raise corn with them.[6]

"That still small voice . . . whispered consolation to my soul"

While confined in prison for six months, Joseph was comforted by the still small voice of the Holy Ghost. This tactic to relieve stress can be practiced by all. A life worthy of the companionship of the Holy Ghost is filled "with hope and perfect love, which love endureth by diligence unto prayer" (Moroni 8:26). Of the period spent in prison, Joseph wrote:

> Death stared me in the face, and . . . my destruction was determined upon, as far as man was concerned; yet, from my first entrance into the camp, I felt an assurance, that I with my brethren and our families should be delivered.

Yes, that still small voice which has so often whispered consolation to my soul, in the depth of sorrow and distress, bade me be of good cheer, and promised deliverance, which gave me great comfort.[7]

Do we worship Joseph Smith?

Some contend that the Church puts undue stress upon the members because of the injunction of the Savior: "Be ye therefore perfect, even as your Father which is in heaven is perfect" (Matthew 5:48).

However, the intention of the Church and the Lord is to promote happiness and contentment, not stress or feelings of failure for not being considered perfect. Joseph taught us perfection was a process, and openly admitted he had faults. We can learn from his example.

Some have asked, do members of The Church of Jesus Christ of Latter-day Saints worship Joseph Smith? The answer is simple: No! We do not worship him. We worship God the Eternal Father, his Son Jesus Christ, and the Holy Ghost. They, as members of the Godhead, are perfect in their righteousness.

While we do not worship Joseph, we certainly honor and revere him, and sustain him as the Prophet, Seer, and Revelator of the last, great dispensation of time. As such he must be considered one of the most noble men ever to live upon this earth. Nevertheless, though he was a good man, Joseph was not perfect. Near the end of his life, he said: "I never told you I was perfect—but there is no error in the revelations which I have taught."[8]

Therefore, Church members are not asked to sustain Joseph as a perfect human being. We are asked, however, to sustain him as the Prophet through whom God chose to restore all things. Brigham Young, who knew Joseph well, gives us the following counsel: "Though I admitted in my feelings and knew all the time that Joseph was a human being and subject to err, still it was none of my business to look after his faults. . . . It was not for me to question whether Joseph was dictated by the Lord at all times and under all circumstances or not. . . . He was called of God. . . . He was God's servant, and not mine."[9]

Lorenzo Snow, who became the fifth President of the Church, is reported to have said that he "observed some imperfections in the Prophet Joseph Smith, but it was marvelous to see how the Lord could still use Joseph in his imperfections. Seeing this, President Snow added that this gave him courage 'that there might be some hope for me.' "[10] We would be wise to follow the same counsel and help others to do the same.

In the last few days before the martyrdom, Joseph expressed his empathy with those who might struggle to understand him: "No man knows my history. I cannot tell it: I shall never undertake it. I don't blame any one for not believing my history. If I had not experienced what I have, I would not have believed it myself."[11]

Those who can help relieve stress

Joseph taught us that those who can most often bring peace to our souls and relieve the tensions of the day are those closest to us, such as spouses, family, and friends. He gave several examples of his feelings in these beautiful expressions:

Reflecting upon the love and faithfulness of his beloved wife, Emma, he said: "Oh what a commingling of thought filled my mind for the moment, again she is here, even in the seventh trouble—undaunted, firm, and unwavering—unchangeable, affectionate Emma!"[12]

Of his loyal brother Hyrum he noted: "What a faithful heart you have got! Oh may the Eternal Jehovah crown eternal blessings upon your head, as a reward for the care you have had for my soul!"[13]

He commented specifically about his long-term friend Newel K. Whitney: "Thou art a faithful friend in whom the afflicted sons of men can confide, with the most perfect safety."[14]

And listing a number of other men who had cared for him in time of need, he said: "My heart feels to reciprocate the unwearied kindnesses that have been bestowed upon me by these men. They are men of noble stature, of noble hands, and of noble deeds; possessing noble, and daring, and giant hearts and souls."[15]

"Joseph Smith Healing at Nauvoo," by Gary E. Smith.
Used by permission of the artist.

17

Temple Work and Genealogy

The Church is not fully organized, in its proper order, and cannot be, until the Temple is completed, where places will be provided for the administration of the ordinances of the Priesthood.[1]

—Joseph Smith

"It is my will that you should build a house"

On June 1, 1833, the Lord commanded Joseph to "build a house, in the which . . . I design to endow those whom I have chosen with power from on high" (D&C 95:8). Joseph discussed this with the brethren. Because of their poor circumstances, most felt that they would build a simple meetinghouse. Joseph's mother records:

Some were in favor of building a frame house, but others were of a mind to put up a log house. Joseph reminded them that they were not building a house for a man, but for God; "and shall we, brethren," said he, "build a house for our God, of logs? No, I have a better plan than that. I have a plan of the house of the Lord, given by himself; and you will soon see by this, the difference between our calculations and his idea of things![2]

The Lord then gave Joseph the directions on how to build his house, just as he had instructed Moses to build the tabernacle in the wilderness, Noah the ark, Solomon the great temple in Jerusalem, and Nephi a boat to sail to the promised land. Hence the Lord said, "Let the house be built, not after the manner of the world. . . . Let it be built after the manner which I shall show unto three of you." (D&C 95:13–14.)

The Lord revealed to Joseph and his counselors in vision how to build his temple.

> Truman O. Angell, one of the supervisors of temple con-struction, testified that the Lord's promise to show the building's design to the Prophet was literally fulfilled. On an occasion when Joseph Smith invited his counselors in the First Presidency to kneel with him in prayer, the building appeared before them in vision. "After we had taken a good look at the exterior, the building seemed to come right over us." Later while speaking in the completed temple, Frederick G. Williams testified that the hall in which they were convened coincided in every detail with the vision given to the Prophet.[3]

The command to build came at a time when the Saints were few and poor, and when to raise the immense sum required meant a great deal of sacrifice on their part. But the Lord said: "It is my will that you should build a house. If you keep my commandments you shall have power to build it." (D&C 95:11.) And build it they did!

First, they needed a construction supervisor to take charge of the work. Since there were few skilled workers among the Saints, Joseph asked if anyone knew of a person capable of overseeing such an important task:

> Lorenzo Young exclaimed to the Prophet, "I know the very man who is capable of doing this work!" "Who is he?" asked the Prophet. Lorenzo replied, "[It] is Artemus Millet. [He was a successful builder in Canada.]
>
> The Prophet turned to Brigham and said, "I give you a mission to go to Canada and baptize Brother Artemus Millet, and bring him here. Tell him to bring a thousand dollars with him."

As strange as it may seem to the unbeliever, Brigham Young went to Canada, found Artemus Millet, taught him the gospel, and baptized him. Within a short period of time, Artemus Millet sold his property, moved to Kirtland with his family, bringing more than a thousand dollars to help with the temple construction, and took over the temple building assign-ment as requested.[4]

Second, the Saints needed workers and funds to pay for the materials. A sandstone quarry was located within two miles of the site, and large stones were removed from there in rectangular blocks for the foundation and walls of the building. Many other materials were donated or seemed to miraculously appear when needed for the work to continue. Each Saint in the area agreed to donate every seventh day to the Lord for the building of the temple, but most spent every spare minute and donated every piece of glass or jewelry for the "House of the Lord."

Where the workers came from was perhaps the greatest miracle. Lucy Mack Smith says that when the work started there were "not thirty families of Saints now remain[ing] in Kirtland." Most had already moved to Missouri. Recently baptized converts from Canada and the East joined in the effort. Sister Smith continues, "How often I have parted every bed in the house for the accommodation of the brethren, and then laid a single blanket on the floor for my husband and myself, while Joseph and Emma slept upon the same floor, with nothing but their cloaks for both bed and bedding."[5]

The sisters devoted their time to feeding the workers, making clothing, and mending and washing the clothing to keep the work moving. Joseph's history reads: "I . . . pronounced a blessing upon the sisters, for their liberality in giving their services so cheerfully."[6]

In 1836, less than three years after the work had started, the Kirtland Temple was completed. The Lord was true to his promise: "It is my will that you should build a house. If you keep my commandments you shall have power to build it." (D&C 95:11.)

"Establish a house, even a house of prayer, a house of learning, a house of glory, a house of God"

On Sunday, March 27, 1836, after three years of sacrifice, the day of dedication had come. Some five or six hundred Saints were there before the doors were open at seven o'clock in the morning. The temple could hold almost a thousand Saints, but the congregation was so large that all could not get in. This made some of the Saints angry, and Frazier Eaton, who had paid seven hundred dollars toward construction, apostatized because he could not get a seat for the meeting.[7]

The Saints came fully trusting the promise of the Lord—"My glory shall be there, and my presence shall be there" (D&C 94:8). They were not disappointed. During the ceremonies of the dedication, for example, an angel appeared and many saw him as he sat between Joseph Smith, Sr., and Frederick G. Williams.[8]

The dedicatory prayer (D&C 109) was given by revelation to the Prophet. Some may have been upset to see him read the prayer, but it is a remarkable prayer which can be studied profitably, in connection with how Saints everywhere can ask for the blessing of heaven upon their own homes and families. It encourages us to "seek learning even by study and also by faith" (v. 7); and to "organize yourselves; prepare every needful thing, and establish a house, even a house of prayer, a house of fasting, a house of faith, a house of learning, a house of glory, a house of order, a house of God" (v. 8). So we "may grow up in thee, and receive a fulness of the Holy Ghost . . . and be prepared to obtain every needful thing" (v. 15).

A further dedicatory meeting and special meetings involving spiritual manifestations continued for several days, and even weeks. One day, as Elder George A. Smith rose to prophesy, a noise was heard like the sound of a rushing wind. All of the congregation arose, and many began to speak in tongues and prophesy. Joseph recorded: "The Temple was filled with angels, which fact I declared to the congregation. The people of the neighborhood came running together (hearing an unusual sound within, and seeing a bright light like a pillar of fire resting upon the Temple), and were astonished at what was taking place. This continued until the meeting closed at eleven p.m."[9]

The visit of Jehovah, Moses, Elias, and Elijah

The Kirtland Temple was not built to serve the same purpose as other temples in the last dispensation. It was built as the place where "the Son of Man might have a place to manifest himself to his people" (D&C 109:5).

There were no special baptismal fonts for baptisms for the dead, no ordinance rooms, no endowment rooms, no sealing rooms. This was the special temple built to receive the keys of the last dispensation and to afford the Saints a special spiritual endowment.

The Lord didn't wait long to restore these precious keys, long held in the heavens waiting for this great day to arrive. On Sunday, April 3, 1836, a congregation of about one thousand gathered to partake of the sacrament. Joseph, his counselors, and the Twelve officiated in the sacred ordinance. After the sacrament, Joseph and Oliver Cowdery dropped the veils around the pulpit and knelt in solemn prayer. The following vision opened to them:

> We saw the Lord standing upon the breastwork of the pulpit, before us; and under his feet was a paved work of pure gold. . . .
>
> His eyes were as a flame of fire; the hair of his head was white like the pure snow; his countenance shone above the brightness of the sun; and his voice was as the sound of the rushing of great waters, even the voice of Jehovah, saying:
>
> Behold, your sins are forgiven you. . . .
>
> . . . Let the hearts of all my people rejoice, who have . . . built this house to my name.
>
> For behold, I have accepted this house. . . .
>
> Yea, I will appear unto my servants, and speak unto them with mine own voice. . . .
>
> Yea the hearts of thousands and tens of thousands shall greatly rejoice in consequence of the blessings which shall be poured out. . . .
>
> And the fame of this house shall spread to foreign lands; and this is the beginning of the blessing which shall be poured out upon the heads of my people. (D&C 110: 2–3, 5–10.)

> After this vision closed, the heavens were again opened unto us; and Moses appeared before us, and committed unto us the keys of the gathering of Israel from the four parts of the earth [missionary work]. . . .
>
> After this, Elias appeared, and committed the dispensation of the gospel of Abraham, saying that in us and our seed all generations after us should be blessed [perfecting the Saints].
>
> After this vision had closed, another great and glorious vision burst upon us; for Elijah the prophet, who was taken to heaven without tasting death, stood before us, and said:
>
> Behold, the time has fully come, which was spoken of by the mouth of Malachi—testifying that he [Elijah] should

be sent, before the great and dreadful day of the Lord come—To turn the hearts of the fathers to the children, and the children to the fathers, lest the whole earth be smitten with a curse [redeeming the dead]. (D&C 110:11–15.)

Thus all the "priesthood keys" of the last dispensation were committed to Joseph Smith, so he could start the great work which would prepare the earth for the second coming of Jesus Christ. Therefore, the Church's mission—to "invite all to come unto Christ" (D&C 20:59) "and be perfected in him" (Moroni 10:32)—has three dimensions:
  1. Proclaim the gospel
  2. Perfect the Saints
  3. Redeem the dead

"We never began to build a Temple without the bells of hell beginning to ring"

"The erection of the Temple at Kirtland seemed to increase the hostile opposition to which the Church had been subjected since its organization; and persecution soon became so violent that all of the Saints who could dispose of their property and leave did so and joined their fellow religionists in Missouri. Within two years following the dedication, a general exodus of the Saints had taken place, and the Temple soon fell into the hands of the persecutors."[10]

When the Saints arrived in the Salt Lake Valley, Brigham Young announced that the Lord wanted them to build another temple. Some of the people complained. In 1861, Brigham Young said:

Some say "I do not like to do it, for we never began to build a Temple without the bells of hell beginning to ring." I want to hear them ring again. . . .

I can say, for my comfort and consolation, and for yours too, that we did build two temples, and commenced another. We completed a temple in Kirtland and in Nauvoo; and did not the bells of hell toll all the time we were building them? They did, every week and every day.[11]

Earlier, in 1853, Brigham Young had said:

It is for us to do those things which the Lord requires at our hands, and leave the result with Him. It is for us to labor with a cheerful good will; and if we build a temple that is worth a million of money, and it requires all our time and means, we should leave it with cheerful hearts, if the Lord in His providence tells us so to do. . . . We should abandon it with as much cheerfulness of heart as we ever enjoy a blessing.

It is no matter to us what the Lord does, or how He disposes of the labor of His servants. But when He commands, it is for His people to obey. We should be as cheerful in building this temple, if we knew beforehand that we should never enter into it when it was finished, as we would though we knew we were to live here a thousand years to enjoy it.[12]

"The Church is not now organized in its proper order, and cannot be until the Temple is completed"

"Now brethren," Joseph had promised, "I obligate myself to build as great a temple as ever solomon did if the church will back me up. Moreover it shall not impoverish any man but enrich thousands."[13]

Obviously the Prophet was speaking in eternal terms, for the temple-building was made possible by the sacrifices made by faithful Saints who gave a tenth of their time and often of their meager income, with larger contributions by some who had greater means. The temple is estimated to have cost $200,000, a huge sum for those days.[14]

Joseph saw in vision what the Nauvoo Temple should look like, and when architect William Weeks brought him the plans, Joseph asked where the round windows were that should be between the first and second floors to let light stream into the temple. Weeks protested that structurally he thought it impossible to put round windows in that place, for they could not bear the weight of the building above them. To this Joseph answered that he had seen the round windows in the vision, and that that was the way the Lord wanted it to be. They had to find a way to do it.[15]

The Lord said that until the temple was built, there was no place on earth where he could come and restore the fulness of the priesthood (see D&C 124:28). "For," said the Lord, "I deign to reveal unto my church things which have been kept hid from before the foundation of the world" (D&C 124:41). Speaking to the Relief Society sisters, Joseph said, "The Church is not now organized in its proper order, and cannot be until the Temple is completed."[16]

To the Twelve he had said several years before, "You need an endowment, brethren, in order that you may be prepared and able to overcome all things."[17] The context of this comment was the then future spiritual outpouring associated with the Kirtland Temple dedication. Elder Boyd K. Packer explained: "The sacrifice the Saints had made to build [the Kirtland Temple], the spiritual power they had built in the process, and their continued ardent desires to do the Lord's will had fitted them for the spiritual manifestations which would "endow [them] with power from on high" (D&C 95:8). When the Saints were empowered by those manifestations, the missionaries would go forth with new zeal and success to spread the gospel, and their womenfolk at home would have the strength and endurance to match those efforts." He also noted that by that time, 1836, "certain ordinances had been introduced in a limited way which later would form part of the regular temple ordinances."[18]

The temple program had been foreseen since before the beginning of time. President Joseph F. Smith testified: "The Prophet Joseph Smith . . . and other choice spirits . . . were reserved to come forth in the fulness of times to take part in laying the foundations of the great latter-day work, including the building of the temples and the performance of ordinances therein for the redemption of the dead" (D&C 138:53–54).

The Nauvoo Temple was under construction from 1841 until 1846. After the martyrdom of the Prophet the Saints felt such anxiety about completing the temple and receiving their ordinances that instead of stopping work on the temple, they increased their labors. Different parts of the temple were dedicated separately as completed, so that ordinance work could begin. As pressure from their enemies increased, so did the Saints' anxiety to receive their temple blessings, and temple work was performed virtually round the clock until they were forced to leave Nauvoo. Brigham Young said: "Such has been the anxiety manifested by the saints to receive the ordinances [of the Temple], and such the anxiety on our part to administer them, that I have given myself up entirely to the work of the Lord in the Temple night and day, not taking more than four hours sleep, upon an average, per day, and going home but once a week."[19]

Joseph and Hyrum did not live to see the temple completed. Yet one can say that they gave their lives so that we might enjoy the hope of eternal life as families.

How many temples will be built

Joseph never said how many temples would be built, but his vision was passed on to Brigham Young, who said:

To accomplish this work there will have to be not only one temple, but thousands of them, and thousands and tens of thousands of men and women will go into those temples and officiate for people who have lived as far back as the Lord shall reveal. If we are faithful enough to go back and build that great temple which Joseph has written about, and should the Lord acknowledge the labor of His servants, then watch, for you will see somebody whom you have seen before, and many of you will see him whom you have not seen before [Joseph Smith], but you will know him as soon as you see him.[20]

Our greatest responsibility

Joseph was told at least four times by the angel Moroni that the last dispensation would require a tremendous work for the redemption of the dead: "Behold, I will reveal unto you the Priesthood, by the hand of Elijah the prophet, before the coming of the great and dreadful day of the Lord. And he shall plant in the hearts of the children the promises made to the fathers, and the hearts of the children shall turn to their fathers. If it were not so, the whole earth would be utterly wasted at his coming." (Joseph Smith—History 1:38–39.)

Why is the genealogical work for the dead so important? The Lord has made repeated statements that "except a man be

born again" (i.e., baptized, which is the key to the celestial
kingdom) and receive the "new and everlasting covenant of
marriage" (i.e., temple sealing, which is the key to exaltation),
he cannot become a god, but must be content, at best, with
being an angel forever. Joseph, speaking to the Relief Society
sisters, said, "The Church is not now organized in its proper
order, and cannot be, until the Temple is completed."[21] To the
Apostles he said, "You need an endowment, brethren, in order
that you may be prepared and able to overcome all things."[22]
Joseph Smith said:

> The greatest responsibility in this world that God has
> laid upon us is to seek after our dead. The apostle says,
> "They without us cannot be made perfect" [see Hebrews
> 11:40]; for it is necessary that the sealing power should be
> in our hands to seal our children and our dead for the ful-
> ness of the dispensation of times—a dispensation to meet
> the promises made by Jesus Christ before the foundation of
> the world for the salvation of man.

> Now, I will speak of them. I will meet Paul half way. I
> say to you, Paul, you cannot be perfect without us. It is
> necessary that those who are going before and those who
> come after us should have salvation in common with us;
> and thus hath God made it obligatory upon man. Hence,
> God said, "I will send you Elijah the prophet before the
> coming of the great and dreadful day of the Lord: he shall
> turn the heart of the fathers to the children, and the heart
> of the children to their fathers, lest I come and smite the
> earth with a curse."

> I have a declaration to make as to the provisions which
> God hath made to suit the conditions of man—made from
> before the foundation of the world. What has Jesus said?
> All sins, and all blasphemies, and every transgression, ex-
> cept one, that man can be guilty of, may be forgiven; and
> there is a salvation for all men, either in this world or the
> world to come, who have not committed the unpardonable
> sin, there being a provision either in this world or the world
> of spirits.

> Hence God hath made a provision that every spirit in
> the eternal world can be ferreted out and saved unless he
> has committed that unpardonable sin which cannot be re-
> mitted to him either in this world or the world of spirits.
> God has wrought out a salvation for all men, unless they

have committed a certain sin; and every man who has a friend in the eternal world can save him, unless he has committed the unpardonable sin. And so you can see how far you can be a savior.[23]

What promises are made in relation to the subject of the salvation of the dead? and what kind of characters are those who can be saved, although their bodies are mouldering and decaying in the grave? When His commandments teach us, it is in view of eternity; for we are looked upon by God as though we were in eternity; God dwells in eternity, and does not view things as we do.[24]

Genealogy, the great welding power

Early in 1841 Joseph was given permission to perform baptisms for the dead at a special place along the Mississippi River not far from Nauvoo. Joseph wrote an epistle regarding baptism for the dead (Doctrine and Covenants section 128), since "that subject seems to occupy my mind, and press itself upon my feelings the strongest, since I have been pursued by my enemies" (v. 1).

The letter referred to several great scriptures. The vision of John, the Revelator, on the Isle of Patmos: "And I saw the dead, small and great, stand before God; and the books were opened; and another book was opened, which is the book of life; and the dead were judged out of those things which were written in the books, according to their works" [Revelation 20:12]. And the great promise to Peter: "Thou art Peter. . . . And I will give unto thee the keys of the kingdom of heaven; and whatsoever thou shalt bind on earth shall be bound in heaven; and whatsoever thou shalt loose on earth shall be loosed in heaven." (Matthew 16:18–19.)

Joseph emphasized the importance of Church records, saying, "whatsoever you do not record on earth shall not be recorded in heaven" (v. 8). Then he made it clear that the priesthood to "seal and bind" is the "welding together of dispensations . . . from the days of Adam even to the present time" (v. 18).

Joseph exulted that the heavens and earth had waited for this great day when the fulness of the gospel would be restored to "enable us [the living] to redeem them [the dead] out of their prison; for the prisoners shall go free" (v. 22).

Let the mountains shout for joy, and all ye valleys cry aloud; and all ye seas and dry lands tell the wonders of your Eternal King! And ye rivers, and brooks, and rills, flow down with gladness. Let the woods and all the trees of the field praise the Lord; and ye solid rocks weep for joy! And let the sun, moon, and the morning stars sing together, and let all the sons of God shout for joy! And let the eternal creations declare his name forever and ever. (D&C 128:23.)

Then the Prophet offered to all the Saints his great challenge:

Brethren, shall we not go on in so great a cause? Go forward and not backward. Courage, brethren; and on, on to the victory! Let your hearts rejoice, and be exceedingly glad. . . .
. . . Let us, therefore, as a church and a people, and as Latter-day Saints, offer unto the Lord an offering in righteousness; and let us present in his holy temple . . . a book containing the records of our dead, which shall be worthy of all acceptation. (D&C 128:22, 24).

18

Testimony of God

*Ye are blessed, for the testimony which ye have borne is
recorded in heaven for the angels to look upon; and they
rejoice over you, and your sins are forgiven you.*
—D&C 62:3

"I had seen a vision; I knew it,
and I knew that God knew it"

It caused me serious reflection then, and often has
since, how very strange it was that an obscure boy, of a little
over fourteen years of age, and one, too, who was doomed
to the necessity of obtaining a scanty maintenance by his
daily labor, should be thought a character of sufficient importance to attract the attention of the great ones of the
most popular sects of the day, and in a manner to create in
them a spirit of the most bitter persecution and reviling.
But strange or not, so it was, and it was often the cause of
great sorrow to myself.

However, it was nevertheless a fact that I had beheld a
vision. I have thought since, that I felt much like Paul, when
he made his defense before King Agrippa, and related the
account of the vision he had when he saw a light, and heard
a voice; but still there were but few who believed him; some
said he was dishonest, others said he was mad; and he was
ridiculed and reviled. But all this did not destroy the reality
of his vision. He had seen a vision, he knew he had, and all
the persecution under heaven could not make it otherwise;
and though they should persecute him unto death, yet he
knew, and would know to his latest breath, that he had both
seen a light and heard a voice speaking unto him, and all
the world could not make him think or believe otherwise.

159

So it was with me. I had actually seen a light, and in the midst of that light I saw two Personages, and they did in reality speak to me; and though I was hated and persecuted for saying that I had seen a vision, yet it was true; and while they were persecuting me, reviling me, and speaking all manner of evil against me falsely for so saying, I was led to say in my heart: Why persecute me for telling the truth? I have actually seen a vision; and who am I that I can withstand God, or why does the world think to make me deny what I have actually seen? For I had seen a vision; I knew it, and I knew that God knew it, and I could not deny it, neither dared I do it; at least I knew that by so doing I would offend God, and come under condemnation. (Joseph Smith—History 1:23–25.)

"*I am a witness that there is a God,*
for I saw Him in open day"

The Prophet bore testimony many times of the sacred experience in the grove in 1820, where he talked with God the Father and Jesus Christ, his Son. One such experience is recorded by Edward Stevenson in his journal:

The Prophet Joseph Smith [was] a plain but noble looking man of large frame and about six feet high. . . . The meetings held were crowded to see and hear the testimonies given, which were very powerful. I will here relate my own experience on the occasion of a meeting in our old log schoolhouse. The Prophet stood at a table, for the pulpit, where he began relating his vision, and before he got through, he was in the midst of the congregation with uplifted hand. I do believe that there was not one person present who was not [convinced] of the truth of his vision of an angel [coming] to him. His countenance seemed to me to assume a heavenly whiteness and his voice was so piercing and forcible—for my part, it so impressed me as to become indelibly imprinted on my mind. . . .

. . . Here are some of the Prophet's words, as uttered in the schoolhouse. With uplifted hand he said, "I am a witness that there is a God, for I saw Him in open day, while praying in a silent grove, in the spring of 1820." He further testified that God, the Eternal Father, pointing to a separate personage, in the likeness of Himself, said, "This is my beloved Son; hear ye Him."

O how these words thrilled my entire system, and filled me with joy unspeakable—to behold one who, like Paul the apostle of olden time, could with boldness testify that he had been in the presence of Jesus Christ![1]

"I saw two glorious personages"

In a letter of March 1, 1842, to John Wentworth, the editor of the *Chicago Democrat*, Joseph wrote of the First Vision as follows:

> Believing the word of God, I had confidence in the declaration of James—"If any of you lack wisdom, let him ask of God, that giveth to all men liberally, and upbraideth not; and it shall be given him." I retired to a secret place in a grove, and began to call upon the Lord; while fervently engaged in supplication, my mind was taken away from the objects with which I was surrounded, and I was enwrapped in a heavenly vision, and saw two glorious personages, who exactly resembled each other in features and likeness, surrounded with a brilliant light which eclipsed the sun at noonday. They told me that all religious denominations were believing in incorrect doctrines, and that none of them was acknowledged of God as His Church and kingdom: and I was expressly commanded to "go not after them," at the same time receiving a promise that the fullness of the Gospel should at some future time be made known unto me.[2]

There was not one who dared to dispute it

Joseph was much like Paul of old who said: "I am not ashamed of the gospel of Christ; for it is the power of God unto salvation to every one that believeth" (Romans 1:16).

Joseph bore his testimony often of the First Vision although he tried not to bring attention to himself as much as to the message. He wanted the listeners to believe in Christ—not in Joseph, the man. On another occasion, Edward Stevenson recorded a statement concerning the testimony offered by the Prophet:

> I first saw him at Pontiac, Michigan, in 1834. . . . He testified with great power concerning the visit of the Father and the Son, and the conversation he had with them. Never before did I feel such power. Though only a small percentage of those who saw and heard him accepted the restored gospel, there was not one who dared to dispute it.[3]

"This is the testimony, last of all, which we give of him: that he lives, for we saw him"

The Prophet and Sidney Rigdon were privileged to see Jesus Christ.

> And while we meditated upon these things, the Lord touched the eyes of our understandings and they were opened, and the glory of the Lord shone round about.
>
> And we beheld the glory of the Son, on the right hand of the Father, and received of his fulness;
>
> And saw the holy angels, and them who are sanctified before his throne, worshiping God, and the Lamb, who worship him forever and ever.
>
> And now, after the many testimonies which have been given of him, this is the testimony, last of all, which we give of him: That he lives!
>
> For we saw him, even on the right hand of God; and we heard the voice bearing record that he is the Only Begotten of the Father—
>
> That by him, and through him, and of him, the worlds are and were created, and the inhabitants thereof are begotten sons and daughters unto God. (D&C 76:19–24.)

Philo Dibble, a personal friend of Joseph's who was present while Joseph and Sidney Rigdon received the vision now known as Doctrine and Covenants, section 76, described what happened:

> Joseph would, at intervals, say: "What do I see?" as one might say while looking out the window and beholding

what all in the room could not see. Then he would relate what he had seen or what he was looking at. Then Sidney replied, "I see the same." Presently Sidney would say, "What do I see?" and would repeat what he had seen or was seeing, and Joseph would reply, "I see the same."

This manner of conversation was repeated at short intervals to the end of the vision, and during the whole time not a word was spoken by any other person. Not a sound or motion made by anyone but Joseph and Sidney, and it seemed to me that they never moved a joint or limb during the time I was there, which I think was over an hour, and to the end of the vision.

Joseph sat firmly and calmly all the time in the midst of a magnificent glory, but Sidney sat limp and pale, apparently as limber as a rag, observing which, Joseph remarked, smilingly, "Sidney is not used to it as I am."[4]

Oliver Cowdery's testimony of how God restored the priesthood

Perhaps one of the most difficult moments in Joseph's fourteen years as President of the Church was the excommunication of his old and beloved friend—Oliver Cowdery. For over nine years they had been intimately associated in the ministry and shared some of the most unusual experiences ever enjoyed by mortals.

The Prophet's critics stand baffled at the decline and fall of Oliver Cowdery, who moved to Wisconsin to practice law in April 1838. If Joseph had been a hoax or if the two men had created a conspiracy to deceive their associates and the public, had their stories about the translation of the Book of Mormon and the appearance of divine beings been fabricated, had they deliberately set about to gain power and influence through fraud and misrepresentation, then evidence to this effect would have surfaced at the time Oliver was excommunicated. But the records are devoid of any such evidence.

On the contrary, never, after leaving the Church, did Oliver deny the reality of the things to which he had testified, nor did he ever question the principles expounded by the Prophet Joseph Smith. In fact, a decade after his excommunication, and four years after Joseph's martyrdom, Oliver returned to the Church. He wrote the following statement, believed to be his last testimony, of the wonderful manifestations which brought the authority of God to men on the earth:

> While darkness covered the earth and gross darkness the people; long after the authority to administer in holy things had been taken away, the Lord opened the heavens and sent forth His word for the salvation of Israel. In fulfillment of the sacred scriptures, the everlasting gospel was proclaimed by the mighty angel who, clothed with the authority of his mission, gave glory to God in the highest.
>
> This gospel is the "stone taken from the mountain without hands." John the Baptist, holding the keys of the Aaronic Priesthood; Peter, James, and John, holding the keys of the Melchizedek Priesthood, have also ministered for those who shall be heirs of salvation, and with these administrations, ordained men to the same Priesthoods.
>
> These Priesthoods, with their authority, are now, and must continue to be, in the body of The Church of Jesus Christ of Latter-day Saints. Blessed is the Elder who has received the same, and thrice blessed and holy is he who shall endure to the end.
>
> Accept assurances, dear brother, of the unfeigned prayer of him who, in connection with Joseph the Seer, was blessed with the above ministrations, and who earnestly and devoutly hopes to meet you in the celestial glory.[5]

The Father and the Son
cannot dwell in your heart

On Saturday, April 2nd, Joseph, accompanied by Orson Hyde and William Clayton, journeyed to Ramus to hold a conference with the Saints. . . . On the following day, Sunday, Orson Hyde was the speaker at the forenoon meeting. . . . He told the Saints that "it is our privilege to have the Father and the Son, dwelling in our hearts."

In the afternoon meeting, President Smith stated that he was going to offer some corrections to Brother Hyde's remarks.

"When the Savior shall appear we shall see Him as He is. We shall see that He is a man like ourselves, and the same sociability which exists among us here will exist among us there, only it will be coupled with eternal glory, which glory we do not now enjoy. [Referring to John 14:23, he said:] The appearing of the Father and the Son in the verse, is a personal appearance, and the idea that the Father and the Son dwell in a man's heart is an old sectarian idea and is false."[6]

Some may feel that after the First Vision Joseph understood all that there was to know about God the Father and his Son, Jesus Christ. However, Joseph was given even more understanding as he matured in the knowledge of the Lord, and twenty-three years later he clearly defined the actual nature of the Father, Jesus Christ, and the Holy Ghost in these words: "The Father has a body of flesh and bones as tangible as man's; the Son also; but the Holy Ghost has not a body of flesh and bones, but is a personage of Spirit. Were it not so, the Holy Ghost could not dwell within us." (D&C 130:22.)

What is meant by "no man hath seen God at any time"?

Many felt Joseph Smith was a blasphemer because he said he had seen God the Father and his Son, Jesus Christ; while the Bible says, "No man hath seen God at any time" (1 John 4:12). This seems to make the Bible contradictory when it says that "Enoch walked with God" (Genesis 5:22), and the Lord spake unto Moses face to face" (Exodus 33:11). And in the New Testament times, Stephen saw "the Son of man standing on the right hand of God" (Acts 7:56), and John, in Revelation, describes Christ as "his eyes were as a flame of fire (Revelation 1:14)." These appearances don't necessarily seem to be restricted to prophets, since in Exodus 24:9–10 it states that seventy of the elders of Israel "saw the God of Israel." Also, the Beatitudes promise, "Blessed are the pure in heart: for they shall see God" (Matthew 5:8).

When Joseph was following the instruction of the Lord to correct some of the errors that had been carried over the centuries in the Bible, the Lord clarified as follows the statement attributed to John:

No man hath seen God at any time, *except he hath borne record of the Son* (JST, John 1:19).

No man hath seen God at any time, *except them who believe* (JST, 1 John 4:12).

In fact, the Lord said, "Moses plainly taught . . . the children of Israel in the wilderness, and sought diligently to sanctify his people that they might behold the face of God; but they hardened their hearts and could not endure his presence" (D&C 84:23–24).

In modern times the Lord told Joseph how he could help others to have the privilege of being in the presence of and seeing Jesus Christ: "Verily, thus saith the Lord: It shall come to pass that every soul who forsaketh his sins and cometh unto me, and calleth on my name, and obeyeth my voice, and keepeth my commandments, shall see my face and know that I am" (D&C 93:1).

One such incident happened to John Murdock and Zebedee Coltrin, two missionary companions, who were visiting with the Prophet Joseph. John Murdock recorded the following:

In one of [our] meetings the Prophet told us if we could humble ourselves before God, and exercise strong faith, we should see the face of the Lord. And about midday the visions of my mind were opened, and the eyes of my understanding were enlightened, and I saw the form of a man, most lovely, the visage of his face was sound and fair as the sun.

His hair a bright silver grey, curled in most majestic form, His eyes a keen penetrating blue, and the skin of his neck a most beautiful white and he was covered from the neck to the feet with a loose garment, pure white, whiter than any garment I have ever before seen. His countenance was most penetrating, and yet most lovely. And while I was endeavoring to comprehend the whole personage from head to feet it slipped from me, and the vision was closed up. But it left on my mind the impression of love, for months, that I never felt before to that degree.[7]

Zebedee Coltrin had a similar experience: "At one of these meetings . . . a personage walked through the room from east to west, and Joseph asked if we saw him. I saw him and suppose the others did and Joseph answered that is Jesus, the Son of God, our elder brother."[8]

19

Work

He who doeth the works of righteousness shall receive his
reward, even peace in this world, and eternal life in the
world to come.

—D&C 59:23

"The best hand he ever hired"

In the winter of 1825–26, while preparing himself to receive
the gold plates, Joseph hired out to Josiah Stoal, and worked
on property he owned in Susquehanna County, Pennsylvania.
While there he boarded at the neighboring house of Isaac Hale,
whose daughter, Emma, was a vivacious young woman, above
medium height, with dark brown hair and brown eyes. On
January 18, 1827, she would become Joseph's wife and lifelong
companion.

Later, when Joseph was translating the plates, Joseph
Knight, a prosperous farmer and mill owner of Broome County,
New York, befriended Joseph and provided needed supplies. Joseph and the Knight family became best friends, and the family
was to play a very important part in the history of the Church. In
1862, Joseph Knight, Jr., in a statement given to the Church
Historian, said his father hired Joseph Smith, Jr., as a laborer in
1827. (This probably should read 1826.) The statement said:

> Joseph and I worked and slept together. My father said
> Joseph was the best hand he ever hired. We found him a
> boy of truth. He was about 21 years of age. I think it was in
> November that he made known to my father and I that he
> had seen a vision; that a personage had appeared to him
> and told him where there was a "gold book" of ancient date
> buried, and if he would follow the directions of the angel, he

could get it. We were told it in secret. My father and I believed what he told us. I think we were the first to believe after his father's family.[1]

The Prophet greatly rejoiced in finding these two loyal friends. And they were to be friends to him throughout his life.

"There is always a heroism in the honest, uncomplaining home toil of youth"

Wondrous as had been the vision of the host of heaven and the ranks of Lucifer; exalting as were the communications from the Lord; mighty as was to be the mission of translation; yet Joseph had day by day the humble labors of life to perform. Without a murmur he accepted his lot of toil, working with his hands to aid in the family maintenance, while his mind was busy with eternal truths. There is always a heroism in the honest, uncomplaining home toil of youth; a necessary heroism, indeed, for without the early formed habit of industry for man, the Almighty's purposes concerning mankind would fail. And that heroism is doubly beautiful in the life of Joseph, who knew already his destiny, divinely ordained. Left much to itself in the selfishness of earth, a weaker or an unsustained soul would have wasted its powers in vain dreamings or found its destruction in pride and self-glory.

The sweat of the face, therefore, was at once a necessity and a salutation: a requisite for the family welfare and comfort; a protection from enervating dreams. No husbandman of all that neighborhood was more industrious than he; and, except for the hatred bred against him by false teachers and their followers, no one would have had a better reputation.[2]

To provide an honest living for the family

The early Saints learned the value of hard work. Joseph's family never would have been considered among the wealthy nor the educated, but they were good workers.

"Arrived in Palmyra," says the historian of Wayne county, "the elder Smith [Joseph's father] opened a 'cake and [root] beer shop,' as his sign indicated, and the profits of the shop, combined with occasional earnings by himself and eldest sons at harvesting, well digging, and other common employments, enabled him to provide an honest living for the family. The shop, with its confectionery, gingerbread, rootbeer, and such articles, was well patronized by the village and country youth, and on public occasions did a lively business.[3]

Joseph's mother, Lucy, had a talent for painting oilcloth coverings for tables, stands, and other furniture. She set up a little business from her home which did quite well. She was able to furnish food for the family and helped replenish the household furniture.[4]

"We had the privilege of getting our shins, feet, and toes bruised"

Brigham Young, who had the privilege of attending school only eleven and one-half days, once recalled what it was like to grow up in Vermont and the western frontier:

> Brother Heber [Heber C. Kimball] and I never went to school until we got into "Mormonism." . . . We never had the opportunity of letters in our youth, but we had the privilege of picking up brush, chopping down trees, rolling logs, and working amongst the roots, and of getting our shins, feet, and toes bruised. . . . I learned to make bread, wash the dishes, milk the cows, and make butter. . . . Those are about all the advantages I gained in my youth.[5]

Study and translation of the Bible set the stage for the reception of many revelations

Joseph was a dedicated worker. Once the Book of Mormon was completed and the Church was organized, he undertook the translation of the Bible. He worked tirelessly at his task, over the same period learning step by step what the Lord wanted done with his newly organized Church. A typical comment in his history is: "No month ever found me more busily engaged . . . but as my life consisted of activity and unyielding exertions, I made this my rule: *When the Lord commands, do it.*"[6]

While translating the Bible, Joseph often sought answers to questions that would arise concerning the order, doctrine, and procedures of the ancient Church of Jesus Christ. These questions led him to seek in prayer answers for the organization and procedures of the recently restored Church of Jesus Christ. Over seventy-five of the current sections of the Doctrine and Covenants were received during that time.

Robert J. Matthews, the Church's foremost authority on the Joseph Smith Translation, says, "It was Joseph Smith's study and translation of the Bible that set the stage for the reception of many revelations on the doctrines of the gospel."[7]

Apparently, when the Prophet translated the Bible he was not limited to what was found on the working page in front of him, whether that page was a sheet from the King James Version or a handwritten draft of his own early revision. It seems that the text was a starting point but that the spirit of revelation was always an additional source of information. In the case of the Bible translation, the initial starting point was the King James Version; this source suggested certain ideas, but apparently the Spirit suggested many enlargements, backgrounds, and additional concepts not found on the page.

Thus the term *translation,* when used in reference to Joseph Smith's translation of the Bible, has a broader meaning than it normally does when one thinks of translating languages. To a prophet, a revelation is a more vital and dependable source than a written text.[8]

Parley P. Pratt, who was present during the time when Joseph received several revelations, describes the process:

Each sentence was uttered slowly and very distinctly, and with a pause between each, sufficiently long for it to be recorded, by an ordinary writer, in long hand.

This was the manner in which all his written revelations were dictated and written. There was never any hesitation, reviewing, or reading back, in order to keep the run of the subject; neither did any of these communications undergo revisions, interlinings, or corrections. As he dictated them so they stood, so far as I have witnessed; and I was present to witness the dictation of several communications of several pages each.[9]

Thus we see it was hard work and spiritual readiness that enabled Joseph to receive what is now known as the Doctrine and Covenants. "These sacred revelations were received in answer to prayer, in times of need, and came out of real-life situations involving real people."[10] "In the revelations one hears the tender but firm voice of the Lord Jesus Christ, speaking anew in the dispensation of the fulness of times."[11]

An example of such clarity is the Lord setting his standard of work for faithful members of his Church, when he says:

> For behold, it is not meet that I should command in all things; for he that is compelled in all things, the same is a slothful and not a wise servant; wherefore, he receiveth no reward.
>
> Verily I say, men should be anxiously engaged in a good cause, and do many things of their own free will, and bring to pass much righteousness;
>
> For the power is in them, wherein they are agents unto themselves. And inasmuch as men do good they shall in nowise lose their reward.
>
> But he that doeth not anything until he is commanded, and receiveth a commandment with doubtful heart, and keepeth it with slothfulness, the same is damned. (D&C 58:26–29.)

"Seek learning, even by study and also by faith"

Joseph learned that great knowledge came through personal revelation, but that the Lord would not do all the work. The Lord gave Joseph the plates, but he had to work and pray to translate them. The Lord commanded him to review and correct some errors in the Bible, but Joseph had to read, study, and pray for the ability to complete his "translation of the Bible." Joseph sought to better understand the covenant of Abraham and the Lord helped him obtain the Egyptian papyri containing the record of Abraham. Joseph learned that to inquire meant to ask for more work.

Joseph wrote in a letter: "We never inquire at the hand of God for special revelation only in case of there being no previous revelation to suit the case. . . . It is a great thing to inquire at the hands of God, or to come into His presence; and we feel fearful to approach Him on subjects that are of little or no consequence . . . especially about things the knowledge of which men ought to obtain in all sincerity, before God, for themselves.[12]

"I had some twenty acres to plow"

It has been said that "man's extremity is God's opportunity," or in other words, when man has done all that he can do but still more is called for to complete the work, the Lord may come to his rescue and help him accomplish the task at hand.

One such incident occurred when the Prophet Joseph and Oliver Cowdery needed help to get from Harmony, Pennsylvania, to Fayette, New York, so they could continue the translation of the Book of Mormon. Oliver had written letters to his friend David Whitmer telling him about the progress of the work. David tells the following story:

"Soon after this (the arrival of a letter from Oliver Cowdery) Joseph sent for me to come to Harmony to get him and Oliver, to bring them to my father's house. I did not know what to do. I was pressed with my work. I had some twenty acres to plow, so I concluded I would finish plowing and then go. I got up one morning to go to work as usual, and on going to the field, found between five and seven acres of my ground had been plowed during the night. I do not know who did it, but it was done just as I would have done it myself, and the plow was left standing in the furrow."

This incident was related to Orson Pratt and Joseph F. Smith by David Whitmer, on the 7th of September, 1878, forty years after he had left the Church. It was to him a miraculous evidence, the force of which he never denied.[13]

Was the Smith family lazy and indolent?

Some critics of the Prophet claimed Joseph and his parents' family were lazy and indolent people. Indeed, they did move many times throughout Joseph's short lifetime, in the early years in an effort to better their economic circumstances; however, most people who knew the family claimed them to be honest, hardworking people. In an interview regarding his recollections of his family, the Prophet's younger brother William responded to questions.

"It is said that Joseph and the rest of the family were lazy and indolent."

[William answered] "We never heard of such a thing until after Joseph told his vision, and not then, by our friends. Whenever the neighbors wanted a good day's work done they knew where they could get a good hand and they were not particular to take any of the other boys before Joseph either. We cleared sixty acres of the heaviest timber I ever saw. We had a good place. We also had on it from twelve to fifteen hundred sugar-trees, and to gather the sap and make sugar and molasses from that number of trees was no lazy job.

"We worked hard to clear our place and the neighbors were a little jealous. If you will figure up how much work it would take to clear sixty acres of heavy timber land, heavier that any here, trees you could not conveniently cut down, you can tell whether we were lazy or not, and Joseph did his share of the work with the rest of the boys.

"We never knew we were bad folks until Joseph told his vision. We were considered respectable till then, but at once people began to circulate falsehoods and stories in a wonderful way."[14]

For the benefit of the Saints, the Lord told Joseph the importance of being a good worker and gave some good instruction on how to avoid laziness and keep the mind and body sharp: "Let every man be diligent in all things. And the idler shall not have place in the church, except he repent and mend his ways." (D&C 75:29.) "Cease to be idle; cease to be unclean; cease to find fault one with another; cease to sleep longer than is needful; retire to thy bed early, that ye may not be weary;

arise early, that your bodies and your minds may be invigorated" (D&C 88:124).

Joseph, the "money digger"

Some have called Joseph a money-digger because he went to work for Josiah Stowell (spelled Stoal in *History of the Church*) to search for a silver mine. Undoubtedly, Mr. Stowell had heard the rumors about Joseph's claim to have found the gold plates. He felt that perhaps Joseph could be the answer to his finding the lost treasure. The question is how and why did Joseph get involved in the project? Joseph's mother explained:

> A man by the name of Josiah Stoal came from Chenango county, New York, with the view of getting Joseph to assist him in digging for a silver mine. He came for Joseph on account of having heard that he possessed certain means by which he could discern things invisible to the natural eye.
>
> Joseph endeavored to divert him from his vain pursuit, but he was inflexible in his purpose and offered high wages to those who would dig for him in search of said mine, and still insisted upon having Joseph to work for him. Accordingly, Joseph and several others returned with him and commenced digging. After laboring for the old gentleman about a month, without success, Joseph prevailed upon him to cease his operations, and it was from this circumstance of having worked by the month, at digging for a silver mine, that the very prevalent story arose of Joseph's having been a money digger.[15]

*Only through belief in Jesus Christ and faith
which manifests itself in good works
can men and nations enjoy peace*

The Lord taught Joseph Smith the principles of stewardship and hard work from the very beginning of his study of the gospel. His driving force to go to the Sacred Grove and ask the Lord in prayer which of all churches was true came from the Epistle of James, which also teaches: "Faith without works is dead" (James 2:26).

Joseph was told by the angel Moroni "that he was a messenger sent from the presence of God" to tell Joseph "that God had a work for me to do; and that my name should be had for good and evil among all nations, kindreds, and tongues, or that it should be both good and evil spoken of among all people." (Joseph Smith—History 1:33).

Throughout his life, Joseph taught the principles of stewardship and hard work. He particularly loved the parables of the Savior. On one occasion he remarked:

Men not unfrequently forget that they are dependent upon heaven for every blessing which they are permitted to enjoy, and that for every opportunity granted them they are to give an account. You know . . . that when the Master in the Savior's parable of the stewards called his servants before him he gave them several talents to improve on while he should tarry abroad for a little season, and when he returned he called for an accounting. So it is now. Our Master is absent only for a little season, and at the end of it He will call each to render an account.[16]

Some of the great principles revealed to Joseph in the Doctrine and Covenants or translated by him in the Book of Mormon help us better comprehend the principle of work and stewardship accounting:

• *Can man deceive God?*

I say unto you, can ye look up to God at that day with a pure heart and clean hands? I say unto you, can you look up, having the image of God engraven upon your countenances? (Alma 5:19.)

Or do ye imagine to yourselves that ye can lie unto the Lord in that day, and say—Lord, our works have been righteous works upon the face of the earth—and that he will save you? (Alma 5:17.)

I say unto you, Nay; except ye make our Creator a liar from the beginning, or suppose that he is a liar from the beginning, ye cannot suppose that such can have place in the kingdom of heaven (Alma 5:25).

• *Every man must learn his duty*

>   Wherefore, now let every man learn his duty, and to act in the office in which he is appointed, in all diligence.

>   He that is slothful shall not be counted worthy to stand, and he that learns not his duty and shows himself not approved shall not be counted worthy to stand. (D&C 107: 99–100.)

• *We are under commandment to teach correct principles to others*

>   I give unto you a commandment that you shall teach one another the doctrine of the kingdom.

>   Teach ye diligently and my grace shall attend you, that you may be instructed more perfectly in theory, in principle, in doctrine, in the law of the gospel, in all things that pertain unto the kingdom of God, that are expedient for you to understand. (D&C 88:77–78.)

• *We must be creative*

>   For behold, it is not meet that I should command in all things; for he that is compelled in all things, the same is a slothful and not a wise servant; wherefore he receiveth no reward.

>   Verily I say, men should be anxiously engaged in a good cause, and do many things of their own free will, and bring to pass much righteousness;

>   For the power is in them, wherein they are agents unto themselves. And inasmuch as men do good they shall in nowise lose their reward.

>   But he that doeth not anything until he is commanded, and receiveth a commandment with doubtful heart, and keepeth it with slothfulness, the same is damned.

>   Who am I that made man, saith the Lord, that will hold him guiltless that obeys not my commandments?

>   Who am I, saith the Lord, that have promised and have not fulfilled?

>   I command and men obey not; I revoke and they receive not the blessing.

Then they say in their hearts: This is not the work of the Lord, for his promises are not fulfilled. But wo unto such, for their reward lurketh beneath, and not from above. (D&C 58:26–33.)

• *Everyone is given a stewardship*

While section 104 was specific to the United Order, each of us is a steward over earthly blessings.

It is wisdom in me, therefore, a commandment I give unto you, that ye shall organize yourselves and appoint every man his stewardship;

That every man give an account unto me of the stewardship which is appointed unto him.

For it is expedient that I, the Lord, should make every man accountable, as a steward over earthly blessings, which I have made and prepared for my creatures. (D&C 104:11–13.)

It is required of the Lord, at the hand of every steward, to render an account of his stewardship, both in time and in eternity.

For he who is faithful and wise in time is accounted worthy to inherit the mansions prepared for him of my Father. (D&C 72:3–4.)

• *Celestial blessings come from earthly actions*

If ye are not equal in earthly things ye cannot be equal in obtaining heavenly things; for if you will that I give unto you a place in the celestial world, you must prepare yourselves by doing the things which I have commanded you and required of you (D&C 78:6–7).

• *John the Revelator saw the evaluation of stewardship and faithful service*

I saw the dead, small and great, stand before God; and the books were opened; and another book was opened, which is the book of life; and the dead were judged out of those things which were written in the books, according to their works (Revelation 20:12).

• *The Lord sets the rules, our actions dictate the outcome*

I, the Lord, am bound when ye do what I say; but when ye do not what I say, ye have no promise (D&C 82:10).

For of him unto whom much is given much is required; and he who sins against the greater light shall receive the greater condemnation (D&C 82:3).

• *Obedience to celestial laws earns celestial glory*

He who is not able to abide the law of a celestial kingdom cannot abide a celestial glory (D&C 88:22).

The Prophet Joseph Smith set forth the purpose of the Church when he declared:

It is the bringing of men and women to a knowledge of the eternal truth that Jesus is the Christ, the Redeemer and Savior of the world, and that only through belief in Him and faith which manifests itself in good works, can men and nations enjoy peace.[17]

References

Key to Abbreviations

American Prophet   John Henry Evans, *Joseph Smith, an American Prophet* (Salt Lake City: Deseret Book Co., 1989).

CHC   B. H. Roberts, *A Comprehensive History of The Church of Jesus Christ of Latter-day Saints,* 6 vols. (Salt Lake City: Deseret Press, 1930).

Commentary   Hyrum M. Smith and Janne M. Sjodahl, *The Doctrine and Covenants Commentary,* rev. ed. (Salt Lake City: Deseret Book Co., 1978).

HC   Joseph Smith, *History of the Church of Jesus Christ of Latter-day Saints,* 2nd ed. rev. B. H. Roberts, 7 vols.

Historical Record   Andrew Jenson, *Historical Record,* 9 vols. (Salt Lake City, 1882–1890).

Journal History   Journal History of The Church of Jesus Christ of Latter-day Saints, Church Historical Department.

JD   *Journal of Discourses,* 26 vols. (1851–1886; lithographic reprint, Salt Lake City, 1966).

LDS Hymnbook   *Hymns of The Church of Jesus Christ of Latter-day Saints,* 1985.

Life of Joseph   George Q. Cannon, *Life of Joseph Smith the Prophet* (Salt Lake City: Deseret Book Co., 1986).

LMS   Lucy Mack Smith, *History of Joseph Smith* (Salt Lake City: Bookcraft, 1979).

Martyr   Francis M. Gibbons, *Joseph Smith: Martyr, Prophet of God* (Salt Lake City: Deseret Book Co., 1977).

Millennial Star   *Millennial Star,* 1840–1970 (Manchester and Liverpool, England).

PPP   Parley P. Pratt, *Autobiograph of Parley P. Pratt* (Salt Lake City: Deseret Book Co., 1938).

Restoration	Ivan J. Barrett, *Joseph Smith and the Restoration* (Provo, Utah: BYU Press, 1973).
Stories	Edwin F. Parry, *Stories About Joseph Smith the Prophet* (Salt Lake City: Deseret News Press, 1934).
Teachings	Joseph Smith, *Teachings of the Prophet Joseph Smith,* sel. Joseph Fielding Smith (Salt Lake City: Deseret Book Co., 1938).
The Prophet	Preston Nibley, *Joseph Smith the Prophet* (Salt Lake City: Deseret Press, 1944).
They Knew	Hyrum L. Andrus and Helen Mae Andrus, comp., *They Knew the Prophet* (Salt Lake City: Bookcraft, 1974).
Times and Seasons	*Times and Seasons*—1839–1846 (Nauvoo).
Words	Andrew F. Ehat and Lyndon W. Cook, *The Words of Joseph Smith* (Provo, Utah: Religious Studies Center, BYU, 1980).
Witness	Scot Facer Proctor, *Witness of the Light* (Salt Lake City: Deseret Book Co., 1991).

Chapter 1. Book of Mormon

1. HC 4:461.
2. Life of Joseph, pp. 26–27.
3. LMS, pp. 82–83.
4. LMS, p. 152.
5. LMS, p. 152.
6. Restoration, p. 103.
7. Restoration, p. 104.
8. Preston Nibley, comp., *The Witnesses of the Book of Mormon* (Salt Lake City: Deseret Book Co., 1973), p. 68.
9. Historical Record, p. 217.
10. *The Witnesses of the Book of Mormon*, p. 48.
11. Historical Record, p. 458.
12. Francis W. Kirkham, *A New Witness for Christ in America*, 2 vols. (Independence, Mo.: Zion's Printing and Publishing Co., 1942), 1:227.
13. HC 1:18–19.
14. JD 19:38.
15. *The Witnesses of the Book of Mormon*, pp. 70–71.
16. HC 4:461.
17. American Prophet, p. vii.
18. Millennial Star, 56:132–34.

Chapter 2. Charity

1. Hyrum L. Andrus, *Joseph Smith: The Man and the Seer* (Salt Lake City: Deseret Book Co., 1960), p. 32.
2. JD 17:92.
3. JD 17:92.
4. HC 6:165–66.
5. Words, p. 117.
6. "Bathsheba Smith," *Juvenile Instructor* 27:345 (June 1, 1892).
7. HC 4:605.
8. "Mary Frost Adams," *Young Women's Journal* 17:538.
9. *Ensign*, September 1978, p. 19.
10. HC 3:327.
11. HC 3:268.

Chapter 3. Courage

1. HC 4:23.
2. PPP, pp. 210–11.
3. PPP, p. 187.
4. HC 3:190–91, footnote.
5. HC 3:191, footnote.
6. PPP, pp. 298–99.
7. HC 6:617–18.
8. *The Witnesses of the Book of Mormon*, p. 45.
9. Restoration, pp. 590–91.
10. Restoration, p. 250.
11. Journal History, July 20, 1833, as told by John Taylor in 1848 to George A. Smith and Les Hawkins, and quoted in Restoration, pp. 250–51.
12. "Mary Elizabeth Rollins Lightner," *Utah Genealogical and Historical Magazine*, July 1926, 17:196.

Chapter 4. Death and Funeral Messages

1. HC 6:619–21.
2. HC 6:621.
3. HC 6:619.
4. LMS, pp. 254–55.
5. LDS Hymnbook, no. 30.

6. HC 6:58.

7. JD 18:361.

8. They Knew, p. 26.

9. As quoted by Wilford Woodruff, *Deseret Weekly News,* March 19, 1892, p. 406.

10. Teachings, p. 216.

11. Life of Joseph, p. 478.

12. HC 6:302–17.

13. Teachings, p. 356, footnote.

14. HC 4:556–57, footnotes.

15. HC 4:554.

16. HC 7:575.

17. JD 17:142.

18. *Discourses of Wilford Woodruff,* ed. G. Homer Durham (Salt Lake City: Bookcraft, 1946), pp. 288–89.

Chapter 5. Faith

1. Words, p. 191.

2. HC 3:379.

3. Life of Joseph, pp. 531–32.

4. *Lectures on Faith* 1:7–10, 12.

5. Life of Joseph, p. 528.

6. LMS, pp. 33–36.

7. LMS, p. 313.

8. HC 2:99.

9. HC 2:100.

10. HC 2:95.

11. Orson F. Whitney, *Life of Heber C. Kimball* (Salt Lake City: Bookcraft, 1967), p. 52.

12. HC 2:104.

13. *Life of Heber C. Kimball,* p. 52.

14. HC 2:105.

15. PPP, p. 46.

16. CHC 1:371.

17. JD 13:158.

18. Commentary, pp. 44–45.

19. *Ensign,* October 1974, pp. 5–7.

20. Matthias Cowley, *Wilford Woodruff, History of His Life and Labors* (Salt Lake City: Bookcraft, 1979), p. 39.

21. PPP, pp. 66–67.

Chapter 6. Family Life

1. The Prophet, pp. 44–45.
2. LMS, pp. 81–82.
3. LMS, pp. ix–x.
4. HC 7:470–72.
5. Teachings, p. 134.
6. Millennial Star 56:132–34.

Chapter 7. Friendship

1. Teachings, p. 316.
2. HC 1:88–89.
3. HC 6:546.
4. HC 6:549.
5. HC 6:555.
6. HC 6:616–22.
7. American Prophet, p. 137.
8. HC 5:393–98.
9. JD 3:51.
10. Susan Arrington Madsen, "The Prophet Joseph Smith, A Friend of Children," *Tambuli* magazine, December 1992, pp. 6–7.
11. Martyr, pp. 242–43.
12. Letters from Joseph to Emma, *BYU Studies*, Summer 1971, p. 520.

Chapter 8. Honesty

1. They Knew, pp. 171–72.
2. The Prophet, p. 45.
3. HC 1:89–90.
4. HC 6:566.
5. N. B. Lundwall, comp., *The Fate of the Persecutors of the Prophet Joseph Smith* (Salt Lake City: Publishers Press, 1952).
6. Commentary, p. 343.
7. JD 18:242.

Chapter 9. Kindness

1. Teachings, p. 31.
2. Teachings, p. 240.
3. Life of Joseph, p. 344.
4. LMS, pp. 324–25.
5. William Taylor, in *Young Women's Journal* 17:548.
6. William M. Allred, *Juvenile Instructor* 27:472.
7. They Knew, p. 127.
8. "He Carried Me," *New Era*, December 1992, p. 38.
9. *New Era*, December 1992, p. 38.
10. HC 2:71, 74.

Chapter 10. Leadership

1. Life of Joseph, p. 529.
2. HC 5:411.
3. Words, pp. 116–18.
4. Life of Joseph, p. 20–21.
5. Wilford Woodruff, in address printed in Millennial Star, September 28, 1905.
6. HC 7:229–30.
7. HC 7:231.
8. Benjamin F. Johnson, *My Life's Review* (Independence, Mo.: Zion's Press, 1947), p. 104.
9. Edward W. Tullidge, *Life of Brigham Young* (New York: Tullidge and Crandall, 1876) pp. 115–16.
10. Zina Huntington, as quoted in Edward W. Tullidge, *The Women of Mormondom* (New York: Tullidge and Crandall, 1877), p. 327.
11. JD 15:81.
12. HC 7:232–42.
13. "History of Brigham Young," *Deseret News*, February 10, 1858, p. 386.
14. Andrus, *Joseph Smith: The Man and the Seer*, p. 114.
15. LeGrand Richards, *A Marvelous Work and a Wonder* (Salt Lake City: Deseret Book Co., 1976), pp. 413–14.
16. HC 3:30.
17. Thomas S. Monson, *Favorite Quotations from the Collection of Thomas S. Monson* (Salt Lake City: Deseret Book Co., 1985), p. 43.
18. Thomas S. Monson, *Favorite Quotations*, p. 46.

Chapter 11. Missionary Work

1. HC 4:540.
2. PPP, pp. 48–51.
3. *Church News,* April 1, 1989, p. 14.
4. Roy W. Doxey, *Doctrine and Covenants Speaks,* vol. 2 (Salt Lake City: Deseret Book Co., 1970), pp. 246–47.
5. Life of Joseph, pp. 318–19.
6. Whitney, *Life of Heber C. Kimball,* pp. 265–66.
7. Life of Joseph, p. 319.
8. Whitney, *Life of Heber C. Kimball,* pp. 272–73.
9. Life of Joseph, pp. 319–20.
10. The Prophet, pp. 376–77.
11. HC 4:557.
12. Witness, pp. 78–80.
13. HC 3:200–201.
14. Dan Jones, "The Martyrdom of Joseph Smith and His Brother Hyrum" (*BYU Studies,* Winter 1984), pp. 89, 94.
15. HC 6:601.
16. *Church News,* March 13, 1993, p. 11.
17. JD 4:34.
18. JD 4:35–36.

Chapter 12. Obedience

1. HC 1:316–17.
2. HC 2:170.
3. JD 11:328.
4. Teachings, p. 345.
5. JD 3:283–84.
6. HC 3:175.
7. JD 5:207.
8. JD 5:210.
9. Fawn M. Brodie, *No Man Knows My History: The Life of Joseph Smith the Mormon Prophet* (New York: Alfred A. Knopf, 1945), p. 74, as quoted in Martyr, p. 71.
10. HC 1:54–55.
11. David Whitmer, "An Address to All Believers in Christ," (Richmond, Mo., 1887), pp. 8–9, as quoted in Martyr, pp. 71–72.
12. Teachings, p. 19.
13. HC 1:408.

14. HC 3:204, footnote.
15. HC 3:202–4.
16. HC 3:192–93.

Chapter 13. Physical Appearance and Strength

1. Teachings, pp. 346–47.
2. Life of Joseph, p. 19.
3. Josiah Quincy, *Figures of the Past* (Boston, 1901), p. 321.
4. Historical Record 7:476.
5. As quoted in American Prophet, p. 7.
6. PPP, p. 45.
7. JD 3:51.
8. Andrew Jenson, *Autobiography of Andrew Jenson* (Salt Lake City: Deseret News Press, 1938), pp. 164–65.
9. Jane James, *Young Women's Journal* 16:553.
10. Life of Joseph, pp. 4, 20–21.
11. Emmeline B. Wells, *Young Women's Journal* 16:555.
12. Wendell J. Ashton, *Theirs Is the Kingdom* (Salt Lake City: Bookcraft, 1970), pp. 265–66.
13. Life of Joseph, pp. 19–20.
14. American Prophet, p. vii.

Chapter 14. Prayer

1. HC 4:425.
2. Kirkham, *A New Witness for Christ in America* 1:44.
3. HC 1:108–9.
4. Andrus, *Joseph Smith, The Man and the Seer*, p. 59.
5. LMS, pp. 228–29.
6. Witness, p. 175.
7. HC 1:146, footnote.

Chapter 15. Service

1. Life of Joseph, pp. 385–86.
2. Millennial Star 55:215 (March 27, 1893).

3. Emma Smith to her son, Joseph Smith III, February 1879; in the *Saints Herald*, vol. 26 (October 1, 1879), pp. 289–90.
    4. LMS, p. 135.
    5. HC 1:32–35.
    6. HC 1:71, 75, footnotes.
    7. HC 1:76, footnotes.
    8. LMS, p. 169.
    9. American Prophet, pp. 38, 44.
    10. HC 5:259.

Chapter 16. Stress

    1. They Knew, pp. 79–80.
    2. Stories, pp. 28–29.
    3. CHC 1:521, 528.
    4. American Prophet, p. 9.
    5. PPP, p. 93.
    6. HC 6:150–52.
    7. *The Personal Writings of Joseph Smith*, ed. Dean C. Jessee (Salt Lake City: Deseret Book Co., 1984), p. 443.
    8. Words, p. 369.
    9. JD 4:297.
    10. "Joseph Smith: A Choice Seer." Talk by Elder Neal A. Maxwell, Holladay Regional Conference, December 1986.
    11. HC 6:317.
    12. HC 5:107.
    13. HC 5:108.
    14. HC 5:108.
    15. HC 5:109.

Chapter 17. Temple Work and Genealogy

    1. Teachings, p. 224.
    2. LMS, p. 230.
    3. Richard O. Cowan, *Temples to Dot the Earth* (Salt Lake City: Bookcraft, 1989), pp. 25–26.
    4. Karl Ricks Anderson, *Joseph Smith's Kirtland* (Salt Lake City: Deseret Book Co., 1989), p. 16.
    5. LMS, pp. 231–32.
    6. HC 2:399.

7. Commentary, p. 722.

8. HC 2:427.

9. HC 2:428.

10. James E. Talmage, *The House of the Lord* (Salt Lake City: Deseret Book Co., 1976), p. 102.

11. JD 8:355–56.

12. JD 1:277.

13. Words, p. 418.

14. Boyd K. Packer, *The Holy Temple* (Salt Lake City: Bookcraft, 1980), p. 129.

15. Witness, pp. 180–81.

16. Words, p. 115.

17. HC 2:309.

18. Boyd K. Packer, *The Holy Temple*, p. 129.

19. HC 7:567.

20. JD 3:372.

21. Teachings, p. 224.

22. HC 2:309.

23. HC 6:313–14.

24. Teachings, pp. 356–57.

Chapter 18. Testimony of God

1. Joseph Grant Stevenson, Stevenson Family History, Provo, Utah, 1955, 1:19–21.

2. HC 4:536.

3. They Knew, p. 85.

4. They Knew, p. 68.

5. *The Witnesses of the Book of Mormon*, pp. 55–56.

6. The Prophet, p. 445.

7. As quoted in *Ensign*, January 1993, p. 37.

8. As quoted in *Ensign*, January 1993, p. 37.

Chapter 19. Work

1. The Prophet, pp. 49–50.

2. Life of Joseph, p. 42.

3. American Prophet, p. 29.

4. LMS, pp. 63–64.

5. JD 5:97.

6. HC 2:170.

7. Robert J. Matthews, "*A Plainer Translation*": *Joseph Smith's Translation of the Bible* (Provo, Utah: BYU Press, 1985), p. 256.

8. Robert J. Matthews, *A Bible! A Bible!* (Salt Lake City: Bookcraft, 1990), p. 110.

9. PPP, p. 62.

10. Doctrine and Covenants Explanatory Introduction, p. 2.

11. Doctrine and Covenants Explanatory Introduction, p. 1.

12. HC 1:339.

13. Commentary, p. 73.

14. Millennial Star, 56:132–33.

15. LMS, pp. 91–92.

16. HC 2:23–24.

17. Monson, *Favorite Quotations*, p. 89.